Acknowledgments

My darling Fianna whose innocence and beauty at times single-handedly kept me walking on this path, you are loved very much.

My mother and father for trying so hard and doing the best you could, for standing by me through thick and thin. Without you I wouldn't be here today; my never ending love goes out to you both.

My siblings, Angela, Mark, Siobhan, and Kathy. It brings out a smile when I think of all the great times we have shared as a family—May all your dreams come true!

The Rooney's and the Mcstravick's always have been and always will be such a bright spot in my life. My grandmother who is no longer with us anymore, not a day goes past without her being in my thoughts. My dear friend Geordie who I met when I was four years old in St. Finian's schoolyard, for always having my back on the streets of Belfast.

Abdi Assidi, for all your wisdom; for understanding me when no one else seemed to. You opened up many doors for me and assured me I would survive. Meeting you was a defining moment and a true gift. Your professionalism and authenticity made me believe. You are a real spiritual warrior, my brother.

The wonderful and amazing Penney LeyShon, your miraculous work left me speechless at times. I will be forever grateful for working with such a unique and lovely individual such as yourself. Without you this book wouldn't have happened.

My guardian angel Janice Zwail, for your brilliance and walking me into deeper
realms of healing and light. You just wouldn't let me give up and you gave me the much needed inspiration to write.

The Horse Whisperer, who masterfully cleansed me and give me the strength to make it to the next phase of my journey.

To Bob for always taking my calls and being an excellent mentor and someone who continually helps keep me right-sized.

Bill, for helping me put many of the pieces together and so

much more.

To all my recovery brothers and sisters, you know who you are. And indeed to all the healers, teachers, and wonderful souls I have encountered who have contributed so much toward my evolution—too many to mention.

Cheryl Woodruff, for helping me kick-start this whole project and for guiding me to get things off the ground, along with Nora Reichard.

And of course, my dear editor Anne Dillon, for working so closely and swiftly. Contributing your professional expertise and deep spiritual insight made the whole editorial process much more pleasurable.

And for all the beings who haven't found peace yet—What you seek, you are seeking with.

Dedication

To all who are in search of an authentic life

Testimonial

Adrian Clarke has helped so many through his own life endurances, a sincere person and a man who has faced and dealt with the revealing struggles of the soul.

Penney LeyShone – Healer, Author and Seer.

Foreword
by
Abdi Assadi

Some of what you will encounter in this book will read as fantastical—or weird, strange, or not possible. Whether you believe such things are possible or not is not important. What is important is where you are in your own spiritual process and understanding. It would be wonderful if you find this material useful in your own life and path. If you find some of it too out there or strange, discard that part and take away what you do find to be useful.

As someone who has been a clinician for over three decades and has come across these types of phenomena many times, I can tell you that they do, in fact, exist and, actually, they are more common than one would realize. It's just that we don't have a cultural language for them and, as such, most people endure them in private for fear of being led away by burly men in white coats.

Reading this book I am once again reminded of how much Adrian had to endure: the brutal feeling of intense anxiety and panic attacks, the fear of insanity, the abject terror of death that leads to chronic insomnia as well as episodes of paranormal activity. This total dismantling of self as one imagines it to be are all common symptoms that occur as one's known life is dismantled. To reintegrate after having gone through such experiences is a tough road. On top of that, all that pain and suffering does not automatically guarantee that we are fully awake.

Our egos are tricky critters by definition and as such do not give up the fight easily. The ego can and generally does get a hold of such experiences and feels special. Besides being locked up in an insane asylum, this is the main danger of such experiences. Feeling special is one of the surest ways to know that we are far from the path. It is just another cloak for our damaged egos to hide behind. The pitfalls of experiences that you will read about in this book is the ego thinking it's special—these paranormal experiences are the ultimate temptation on that front.

We are *not* special, and these experiences are *not* a magical panacea. At the end of the day, we are all the same. We have wounds, hopes, gifts, strengths and weaknesses in different measure.

An analogy about paranormal experience might be helpful here. We experience less than .003 percent of the electromagnetic spectrum with visible light. That means that 99.9 percent of the spectrum is invisible to our naked eyes. Read that again: we are basically seeing a very minute amount of what surrounds us at any time. What paranormal experiences do is open up some more percentages that are not usually accessible. It's like radio waves: they are ever-present but we have no knowledge of them unless we have a radio available. When we are in possession of such a device, we can access information in the form of music or news, which we were not able to access before.

Are there people who possess what seem like magical powers, such as "the Horse Whisperer" who you will encounter in this book? Yes, and again they are neither as rare as you might think nor any more special than you. Are there charlatans that act like they have these powers? Oh yes, there are plenty of those as well. The more important takeaway here is not to give one's power over to someone who has or seems to have access to powers that appear to be out of the ordinary.

One should no more or less be in awe of such a person as one would be of a good doctor or surgeon. When needed, they are just the ticket. But that does not necessarily mean that they are balanced human beings or that they are any more enlightened about the affairs of the world than we are.

Adrian is still in process—as are we all. The job of spiritual practice is to humble us and teach us that we are all connected and on the same level. The practice is to smooth out what has not been beaten out of us by life's trials and tribulations. Our only true medicine is to stay in the moment, moment to moment.

Allow everything that you come across, including this book, to guide you to be more true to who you truly are. On the spiritual path we are always beginners. As soon as "we" think "we" got it, the rug gets pulled. After all, the big joke is that the one running after the truth is not real—truth is all there is.

Abdi Assadi, M.S., Lic. Ac. is a spiritual counselor and acupuncturist in his thirtieth year of clinical practice in New York City. His work centers on helping his clients use their disease and dysfunction as a doorway to spiritual serenity. Through his decades of practice, he has learned that identifying and integrating the human shadow—those disowned or repressed puzzle pieces of self that wreak havoc in our lives—offers the most lasting healing for what ails us in body, mind, and spirit. He has studied Chinese, Japanese, and Vietnamese acupuncture, body-centered psychotherapy, external and internal martial arts, and indigenous shamanic practices as well as diverse meditative techniques. He rides motorcycles, curses with abandon, and believes we should live in this transient world as fully as possible.

Preface

I feel so blessed to have walked the path I have walked and remain on—and to have met some of the people I have been blessed to meet. I have the strongest feeling that my journey began many lifetimes ago but somehow I ended up in dear old Belfast in my present body. Then the grips of alcoholism lured me onto the spiritual path; the horrors of entity possession forced me to endure suffering on a level beyond anything I had ever known; and the all-powerful and wonderful, always loving but most merciless Kundalini, exploded and flowed in me like a waterfall of divinity—the master experience of them all. Heaven only knows how many bodies and lifetimes I have been through for these things to occur in this, my present lifetime.

In my times of darkness and struggle I was encouraged by several of my healers to write about what was occurring in my life. They told me it would contribute to my own healing, for there is definitely a healing component in the practice of writing things down. The second reason was so that others may find help in their darkest hours.

As I journeyed into the spirit world with a group of female shamans one night, I was looking for healing and answers. I had the clearest vision that this book would be written, and that its setting would be New York City. In my vision I observed the books being printed on top of a city building and then being distributed through the night's starlit sky. After receiving this very clear and precise vision, I didn't need any more coaxing to write the book.

The moment I sat down on my keyboard and put some sentences on the page a flow began to happen. This would by and large occur every time I set out to write. The toughest part was the battle within me that occurred often, almost like an inner spiritual battle between ego and soul. This took the form of a voice that was continuously trying to deter me from bringing my story to the world, but it was coupled with a desire that wouldn't let me quit. Be that as it may, I often had to shelve the whole endeavor for months at a time as a different part of my Kundalini process would work through me, making it virtually impossible to concentrate on anything but what I was going through physically, mentally, and emotionally.

I am very proud of the fact that I was always able to return to the writing of this book. This has definitely contributed to my own healing in a massive way and squeezed out a tear or two when I was revisiting the past—it's been that much of an emotional experience for me. Before I began writing it, I gave much thought to what would appear on these pages. I was concerned about how its words might affect my life and the lives of my family members. I was concerned about how others would view me after I had revealed myself on such a deep and intimate level. I questioned myself over and over: Will people look at me as some sort of crazy person? Will they believe what I have written? Yet, at the end of the day I didn't care, and why should I, as I speak honestly and from my heart?

I had the deepest intuition and guidance that this story needed to be told so that others who are adrift in the dark, murky waters that this universe sometimes manifests may find a ray of hope and inspiration . . . And that they may come to know they are safe and protected and, wherever they are—they are never walking alone.

Adrian Clarke
2016

Who looks outside, dreams
Who looks inside awakes
Carl Jung

Table of Contents

Chapter 1: The Unfolding
Chapter 2: The Nightmare Accelerates
Chapter 3: Introducing the Irish "Horse Whisperer"
Chapter 4: Early Days in Belfast
Chapter 5: My Excessive Drinking
Chapter 6: A Spiritual Cleansing in Ireland
Chapter 7: Three Healers to the Rescue
Chapter 8: On the Ropes at Work
Chapter 9: The Ego in Its Death Throes
Chapter 10: The Kundalini Ring Brings Everything Full Circle
Chapter 11: Holding Fast While the Karma Continues to Clear
Chapter 12: The Universe Forces My Hand Once More
Epilogue
Appendix: The Seven Chakras
Resources

LIVING HELL – LIVING HEAVEN

By

Adrian Clarke

Chapter One
The Unfolding

November 17, 2010, started out the same as any other day in my life. When I left my apartment that morning, I didn't suspect that the day would become a pivotal point in my life and that I would soon face the biggest challenge I have ever known. In fact, looking back now, I mark November 17, 2010, on the calendar as the day that changed my whole world forever.

That morning, I drove to Astoria Energy LLC, a power plant in Queens, New York, where I was an ironworker—a welder, to be specific. I clocked in at the turnstile and went to the shanty with the rest of the ironworkers to prepare for another day's work. On the site, we had already erected a structural staircase and connected the steel, and I was now doing what welding needed to be done. At around 9:30, my coworkers and I gathered for our morning coffee before making our way back to the shanty.

A stack of steel I beams obstructed my pathway, and I proceeded to climb over them, not realizing that the steel was wet. In a moment I had slipped and lost my balance. I went down on my left knee then over the top of the steel beams and down onto the ground. As I landed, I felt a crack at the base of my spine and an instant pain, coupled with another very strange sensation. I knew I had done some kind of damage, but being a thickheaded Irishman, I tried to ignore it as I finished my break. I mentioned to my coworkers what had happened, then tried to return to work. When I positioned myself to resume welding, however, I discovered that I could not perform my duties—the pain shooting from my back was excruciating.

I ended up in Mount Sinai Hospital later that day. And that was the end of work for me for almost an entire whole year. I had been sent to this job four months earlier, in July, by my union delegate. It was the third construction company I had

1

worked for on this site. The construction industry in New York City was hitting a slow spell about this time, so I was just happy to be working, even if it meant jumping from company to company and putting in some evening shifts from time to time.

The key was to keep working. I had been having a nice run and probably had reached the most comfortable living I had known in my entire thirty-six years. Heaven only knows that I had gone through serious struggles up until this point, so this was a welcome period in my life. I had just moved into a new apartment in Queens, and I was driving a nice car. I had gotten out of a marriage I wasn't happy in and was enjoying dating and having fun. I shared custody of my eight-year-old daughter, Fianna, and my relationship with her was flourishing; I was making a good income, I had not been depressed in a while, and I was pretty confident about my life and the direction it was headed. I enjoyed a very healthy lifestyle.

Physically, I was as fit as I had ever been, and I was in the best spiritual condition ever. I was a recovered alcoholic and as such, had actively engaged in 12-step work with various mentors and with other alcoholics who had gotten free of their alcoholism. Initially this was in Belfast, where I got sober in 2001, and then it continued on with work in the United States, where I had moved in 2002. Admitting I had a problem with alcohol was the first piece of this work; conceding this was something I had battled for years. When I made the connection that I was an alcoholic it felt like the gates of hell opened up. The 12-step process, however, gave me the vision to see why I drank the way I did and what needed to be cleared out of the way in order to experience a life free of the bottle. I had been set on my way with what was a very valuable spiritual program for someone who had a bad drinking problem. It was the first real piece of spiritual work I had ever done and it soon became an invaluable way of life for me. As a member of this fellowship I was doing everything that my recovery program asked of me and reaping nice rewards for so doing.

I would have said I was very happy, and I was excited about

what life was going to offer up next. At least that's what I thought back then. What I had really found was some peace. I wasn't to know what true happiness was for many a day. All that said, the one thing about life you can count on is its unpredictability. While I often have certain ideas and expectations in my head about what the future is going to bring, and while my head will try to convince me it knows what's just around the corner, it's generally not very accurate. Back in November 2010, my mind was definitely a million miles away from the path that my life was about to take over the next several months and years. Actually, I never could have fathomed the many twists and turns of this path I was to travel. I still can't get my head around everything that has happened to me, and I've come to accept that I never really will.

Back then, I thought that my accident on the I beams was nothing more than misfortune and some really bad timing. What was really happening, however, was that this super universe of ours was taking over control of my life in order to prepare me for a series of sometimes brutal, and other times beautiful, experiences. Those amazing experiences are the ones I am going to share with you in this book.

Things were to unfold rather slowly at the end of 2010 and the beginning of 2011. My life at this time, after the accident, was really all about going to doctors' appointments, lying on tables for chiropractic adjustments, doing physical therapy, and trying various types of pain management—all rather boring and frustrating given that I had been used to living a very active life. I had always been involved in sports and had made staying fit a priority by my many visits to the gym. Exercise and activity helped me cope with stress and depression, both of which I had struggled with on and off since I was young.

By early to mid-2011, I was finding it difficult to deal with being partially disabled, and felt as if I had been shipwrecked. Nevertheless, I tried to stay occupied as best as I could and make good use of my time while I was out of work. The plus side was that I didn't have to be on a high-rise building in freezing temperatures or endure being stuck beside the East River while ice-cold winds blew across it. This was the first winter in many years that I had been excused from that detail, and I certainly wasn't complaining about missing out on any of *that*!

I had some savings in my union funds, and I was collecting a check every two weeks from workers' comp insurance, so I could still afford to live; that alone significantly reduced my stress level. Doctors had been advising me to consider surgery to relieve the pain I was experiencing in the lumbar region of my spine, pain that sometimes left me lying on the floor in a heap, like a pretzel. My intuition told me to hold off on having surgery for as long as possible, so I did.

Apart from the pain and discomfort, I was getting by fine and didn't think it would be very long until I returned to work. I even took a trip to Belfast, Ireland, over Christmas to see my family, which was exciting—I hadn't been back there during the holidays for a decade.

I had been born and raised in West Belfast, the youngest of five children. I had three older sisters—Angela, Siobhan, and Kathy—and an older brother, Mark. Kathy had moved to London to pursue her acting career and Mark had moved to New York many years before me and, like myself, was also an ironworker. Angela and Siobhan had both stayed in Belfast and raised their families in Ireland. This was the first time we had all been together for quite some time. The occasion was extra-special as it was the first Christmas we would share in many years, for I had moved to New York to live in February of 2002.

There really wasn't much more to my life during those first months after the accident. Mostly I focused on taking it easy and giving my body a chance to heal. I hoped that I would recover to the point that I could return to my job as an ironworker, which up until then I had been reasonably happy doing. That's what really seemed important to me at the time.

But those days were the quiet before the storm. Life was giving me a break to prepare for what lay ahead.

* * *

It was April 2011—five months after my accident—just around Easter time; the sun was beginning to shine after a long, dark cold New York winter. I awoke in my bed one morning, did a quick mental scan of my body, and automatically sensed a difference. Something had appeared within my being that hadn't been there the day before.

It's really difficult to describe the actual sensation I had: it felt a bit as if a cold energy, almost a slight surge of damp electricity, was trying to settle in around my nervous system. The sensation seemed to be located in a part of me that I hadn't actually been aware of before. As this energy remained, hovering around my nervous system, my mind began to pay more attention to it. It was definitely strange, but I didn't believe it was a cause for alarm. So I did what I do every morning; I said my morning prayers and did my meditation and tried to let whatever it was run its course and leave my system.

I have always been a sensitive person, and over the years I had sought out many different types of spiritual experiences. This, however, was something much different; in fact, at the time, I wasn't viewing it as something spiritual—quite the opposite. It didn't feel uncomfortable, exactly, but it wasn't what I would have labeled as pleasant either. Because it was a very new sensation for me, I can recall that my ego wiggled its way in, slowly at first, trying—thought by thought—to figure out just what this new strange sensation actually was.

Over the next few days and weeks the energy began to feel as if it was percolating, even becoming a little more aggressive. In hindsight, I recognize that a very natural experience was taking place within my body, but at the time, that's just not how my ego was interpreting things. I remember trying to sit with the energy and go into it and basically put to use the spiritual tools I had assembled over time.

However, as I sat with the energy and focused on it, using all the tools at my disposal to eradicate it, the stronger it became. I didn't know it at the time, but the breathing exercises and meditation I was doing were like throwing gasoline on a fire. Soon the energy would begin to rage, and that damp electric feeling would become ever sharper and more jagged, resulting in an even more aggressive energy than before. This energy began to bring about waves of anxiety and I remember feeling that something inside of me was really changing.

I felt a growing uneasiness at this point, about myself . . . and about my life.

Chapter 2
The Nightmare Accelerates

I was driving through Manhattan one Friday evening around this time when my anxiety became so intense that I felt I was facing a fight-or-flight situation. It seemed as if someone had just released a life-size pressure valve in the deepest part of my soul. In that defining moment I was plunged into nearly five years of what often felt like absolute hell as my ego scrambled to figure things out and hang onto everything it thought it knew about keeping me secure and alive.

That's what my ego had done for most of my life. It had tried to protect me with its fear-based solutions, but it had never had to work so hard and so fast before. I fell into terror mode, with tidal waves of anxiety rushing through my body like the howling wind and thoughts racing through my brain at what seemed like hundreds of miles per hour.

Up until this point, my ego had followed a pretty standard pattern. Day by day, as I underwent experience after experience, my ego collected information and data and stored it all in the file cabinets of my brain. Then, when confronted with a new question or problem or issue, it looked for a solution in the files it had already compiled. This was how things had worked all my life.

On that Friday evening, though, my ego didn't know what had hit it. I imagine it frantically searching through every cabinet several times over before finally realizing it had nothing on hand that would guide a proper understanding of the unfamiliar state in which I now found myself.

It's tough to find words to adequately describe the events of that evening and the next morning. I was sliding into a pit of terror, as if someone had pushed me over the side of a cliff and I was free falling, not knowing where—or even when—I would land.

As mentioned earlier, I was an alcoholic in recovery with a past marked not only by alcoholism but by drug use and quite a bit of violence. As such, I had been a dedicated and active member of a recovery program for over a decade. I had been plagued with an obsession to drink alcohol since my teenage years in Belfast, and this obsession had led me down a path self-destruction. By 2011, I considered myself very lucky to have achieved ten years of sobriety—ten years of freedom from my past life. It was an unbelievable milestone that I had found impossible to imagine at the beginning of my journey, which I often refer to as my "conscious spiritual journey." I have watched a great many people come to recovery. A good number of them don't actually make it very long before they return to whatever it was that had hold of them before they walked through the meeting room doors.

One might say that, with the success of this recovery program, I had been granted a new life, or a second bite of the apple. The most amazing aspect of all of this for me was that my obsession to drink booze had long vanished, never to return; this had resulted from a total shift within my being. I don't actually remember the day God removed that burden from me, but he did. In retrospect, it's really amazing to me how an obsession can rule someone's life for decades. Then, all of a sudden, once that individual takes certain actions and begins to live by spiritual principles, that obsession vanishes into thin air, almost as if a spiritual antibiotic had eradicated it.

But the reverse is also true. People with decades of sobriety (if they make it that far) who stop taking certain actions and stop living by spiritual principles—the very process that liberated them—can quickly fall back into the grips of the illness. They pick up a drink once more, and that is an ugly sight to behold. I truly believed I was a guy who was doing the real work and was sincere about it.

And yet on that Friday evening as I was driving through Manhattan, all the fears that I had successfully worked through or had held at bay for so long about my sobriety returned in that one moment of internal explosion. To say the experience threw me for a loop would be an understatement; to say the obsession and desire to drink alcohol returned would be inaccurate. What actually happened was that my ego created the belief that the obsession to drink booze would return if I didn't get things back to the way they had been, and pronto. This was a strange and frightening situation to find myself in.

I have spoken to quite a few people who have had similar experiences, and the ego always seems to conjure up a convincingly scary storyline—employing, for example, the fear of dying––that it replays over and over again. I haven't spoken to anyone who has had the exact experience I had, in which the fear of drinking alcohol showed up. Instead, everyone's own worst personal nightmare would loom its ugly head and make an appearance.

In my case, my ego conjured up the worst possible thing it could: a return to drinking by an alcoholic who had achieved long-term sobriety and had gotten his life together. I was absolutely petrified. I immediately started to worry that the recovery program had run its course, or that I was doing something wrong. I couldn't understand why this would be happening to a guy like me. I had been a good person—well behaved anyway, for the last decade. I had followed the 12-step protocols as best I could; and I had guided lots of others in following them, too. But the turmoil had been set in motion, and I tried desperately to figure out what was happening to me.

I couldn't think straight at all, so I called some friends—just to reach out and talk to those who knew me best, to ensure that I wasn't going crazy. A friend in Pennsylvania was the first person I could get on the phone. When she picked up, I tried to explain to her what was going on. She must have been alarmed to hear my terror-stricken tone; I was blurting out words at a hundred miles an hour. After speaking to me for a while to calm me down, she told me to pack a bag and come to her house in Pennsylvania. Then her husband got on the line to give me directions. I recall going back to Queens, packing a bag, and starting the drive west.

* * *

That night would last a long time in my memory; it's when I went into a severe panic attack that would last for many days. This panic attack set me on a search that took me not only all around the United States and to Ireland but many places beyond—and into the depths of my own soul as well. It sent me into a frenzy to learn what the hell was wrong with me, to understand what was going on. I didn't yet know that I would soon connect with some of the most remarkable healers and people on this planet, and that I would experience a full rewiring of my body and brain.

During the drive to Pennsylvania my head was racing with one crazy story after another and as I tried to process what was happening to me, my ego jumped from one theory to another. At the same time, my body was *filled* with energy; it seemed to be blowing through me like a strong wind. I squeezed the steering wheel tightly, feeling as if I was about to explode, and every twenty seconds or so I would almost lose my breath as I exhaled forcefully through my mouth, trying to release the built-up energy. I couldn't detach from my wildly racing thoughts, and I was *freaking out*—it was all too much; never in my life had I been in such a state before. It was dark and late, but I knew I needed to be around people who I knew well and trusted beyond measure because I was unsure what would happen next.

The drive to Pennsylvania took around two hours, but when I reached the area where my friends lived, my GPS started going haywire and I couldn't find their house. I phoned them repeatedly, but no one answered. This was bizarre—they were expecting me—and it contributed to the fear and confusion I was feeling. Again and again I got their voice mail, and it seemed as if I was driving around in the dark woods of Pennsylvania forever. I finally went to a Wendy's drive-through, hoping one of the kids working there could point me in the right direction, but no one could help. So after driving in circles for what seemed like hours, I turned back toward New York City.

It was now one or two in the morning. I was extremely distressed and riddled with fear and anxiety, not to mention overwhelmed from the torrent of energy I was feeling, which was becoming more and more aggressive. I desperately needed to talk to someone, just to remain sane. I have never felt so alone in my whole life as I did that night. Earlier in the evening I had left messages for several of my friends and during my drive back to the city, they—fortunately—started to return my calls, even though it was the middle of the evening. They clearly understood something was very wrong with me. Suffice to say that I was immensely grateful for their calls during my drive.

My friend Jimmy met me back in New York at around four in the morning. By then my friends in Pennsylvania had called to apologize for our missed connection—they had fallen asleep and not heard the phone (!)—but they wanted me to come back, if I felt up to it, and spend the weekend. Again, I welcomed this invitation. When I reached my apartment, I tried to get a few hours sleep but was unsuccessful; I lay on my bed and watched the sun come up, wondering if I was in the midst of a nervous breakdown. My mental condition that morning was as much torture as I had ever experienced. I simply don't have the vocabulary to describe my condition fully—but the psychological pain was unbearable, and it seemed as if I was being pushed toward insanity or even death.

I did return to Pennsylvania that day, and as I sat on my friends' sofa, I asked myself questions and tried to figure out what was happening to me. Why was I so afraid? Where was this energy coming from? Why did it seem as if it was trying to commandeer my life? What exactly were the sharp electric spasms shooting through me from head to toe?

My weekend in Pennsylvania seemed to last forever, and the energy I felt moving through my body grew even more intense as each hour passed. Between the energy and the anxiety, I didn't know which end was up and it was very obvious to my friends that I wasn't doing well. On top of this, various horrific scenarios were rolling through my mind. The most prominent one was: What if I once again began to drink alcohol or take drugs in order to shut out what was happening to me? I didn't know the answer to that or any of the other questions that were surging through my mind.

I started to feel very grateful for the spiritual training I had undergone over the past ten years in recovery. But I was afraid that it had somehow stopped working or that I had developed a spiritual or mental illness. In addition to the intense anxiety and the over-whelming energy coursing through me, what I felt most was total powerlessness and hopelessness, unlike anything I had ever experienced before.

When the weekend was over and I had returned home to New York, I reached out to various mentors and teachers from my 12-step program to see if they could help. The 12 steps are designed to connect one to a higher power and help relieve one's substance obsession and allow one to live a useful and purposeful life. As the name implies, the program is broken down into twelve guiding principles that offer support in one's recovery process. A 12-step program is comprised of a community of others who are in recovery, and "mentors" who have successfully turned their lives around by following the 12-step principles.

The recovery way of life had totally worked for me for many years. However, now it seemed as if my sobriety could give way at any moment. Actually, to be more accurate, it seemed like my life could end at any moment. Yet I would rather have put a pistol in my mouth and swallowed a bullet than go back to the life I had lived before becoming sober.

And just to be clear, as I went deeper into the 12-step process, my fears about a return to a life of drinking were actually getting *worse*. I didn't want to start drinking again, but my mind kept telling me that I might have to in order to shut off the crazy energy inside me that could not be silenced. Furthermore, and perhaps the weirdest part of the whole scenario, was that another voice was prompting me to shoot heroin, something I had never done or desired to do in my entire life. My head was filled with thoughts—no, more like voices—that were telling me to find a shooting gallery.

These are the demons that I began to do battle with every day.

Revisiting the 12 steps once again in order to find some peace of mind did not offer me comfort. In fact, I seemed to be getting worse instead of better. Nevertheless, I continued to reach out to the teachers and mentors who had been guiding me in a spiritual community, for whatever they had to offer. As my situation became ever more desperate and confusing, I grew increasingly concerned. I started to work with my main mentor to see if we could address what seemed to be a buildup of "life stuff" that just needed to be cleansed. I had all sorts of ideas about what might be triggering what I was going through, but none of my ideas panned out.

By this stage, the fear that I would begin drinking or using drugs again was with me every moment of every day. I could not find a resting place or a moment's quiet anywhere. Between the terror I felt and the unrelenting, overpowering energy coursing through my body, I found myself exhausted but unable to sleep. More than once I so desperately craved rest that I considered checking myself into a hospital of some sort, but I never did. Trying to hold that thought—or any other for that matter—long enough to act on it was impossible.

It was as if internal explosions kept going off and I would get shell-shocked after each one over and over again, which would bring major disorientation. I had to begin living my life moment to moment, since I couldn't predict what would take place from one minute to the next. And I needed to be in the company of someone virtually all the time because I was so freaked out. Practically speaking, however, this was not always possible for I had been divorced for many years and was living alone. All of my family lived in Ireland, except my brother, Mark, whom I didn't see that often, and I didn't have a steady girlfriend at the time.

I knew I had to have faith that the universe would take care of me, but that was difficult to do with the set of circumstances that was unfolding. My internal state was complicated, to say the least, and trying to explain it to others was extremely difficult. More than once people looked at me as if I was crazy. I lived in this condition for a very long time; in fact, years would pass before I started to feel even remotely safe again.

Although I never checked myself into any kind of facility so that I might be able to get some much needed sleep, one of my biggest fears was that I *would* end up in a hospital or a psych ward. I also knew that in a hospital setting I likely would have been diagnosed and given psych meds. I didn't want any of this because deep down, below the frantic energy, anxiety, and the fearful thoughts, I had a strong sense that I was *not* going insane, that there was actually some very real process at work.

During this period I tried to be around close friends only, and even though they didn't understand what was happening to me, they showed up for me fully and tried to help me in every way they could. To this day I feel very blessed to have been graced with such people in my life. I know there were times when I was a total pain in the ass.

The hardest moments were when I was totally alone, lying on my bed, sometimes for days at a time, unable to move from the physical pain and the coursing energy. My thoughts would race as I wondered what was wrong with me. What was causing the wind blowing around and through me? Was the physical pain shooting through my body from my work accident or from something else? I see today that not being with my family during those difficult days and nights was for the best. They would not have understood what I was going through and would have been unable to help me.

Around this time I began to think that perhaps I was in the middle of a prolonged spiritual crisis, for paranormal activity started to take over my life. This created a very tricky terrain for me to navigate each day, and once again I felt as if I was walking a tightrope between sanity and insanity. I thought that if I lost my balance, I would fall into the unknown—that is, if I wasn't there already. Having to deal with the crazy thoughts that were constantly patrolling my mind as well as the relentless energy surging through my body, I didn't know how much I could handle, and it felt as if death was constantly hovering nearby. Amid all my fears was the idea that I might have to end my life if something didn't change, even though a part of me felt I would never take that step. Additionally, I could not bear the thought of leaving my young daughter.

The more my ego tried to figure out these very bizarre goings-on, the more my body filled with terror, and the more powerless I became. Whatever was happening was completely inexplicable. Ego often creates false stories that *appear* to be real problems that need to be figured out, yet really they're all illusory. However, the ego will next attempt to resolve the illusory problems that it has created. Is this insane or what? This process flashed through my mind's eye over and over again.

The energy blowing through my body had by now begun to cause extreme back and neck pain, and I wasn't sure how much longer I would be able to take what felt like bolts of lightning cracking through my head. I worried over and over that I would be forced to seek meds to stabilize me, even though I remained convinced that meds and/or a hospital were not going to be my answer.

I was totally out of ideas about how to resolve my condition, and the not knowing wore on me every second of every day. I thought what I was enduring must be something spiritual in nature, but I had been under the impression that spiritual experiences were accompanied by great feelings of bliss and contentment. And that definitely was *not* how I was spending my days. I continued to closely follow that intuition that guided me away from doctors and hospitals, although not a day passed when I did not, out of desperation, consider the possibility. As well, I still held on to the hope, however small it had become, that one day I would be able to get back to living and enjoying my life again.

* * *

I was now more than a month into this ordeal, and in a very unstable condition. I needed to either be on the phone with someone or in the company of someone constantly. My friends in Pennsylvania were kind enough to continue to open their home to me, and I frequently took advantage of their hospitality, driving back and forth between the city and their house in the country.

We would go out walking together in the countryside, just to see if the change of pace—and the exposure to nature—would help distract me from the coursing energy and the bolts of pain. I recall those days as being a real transitional period, when things went from very bad . . . to hell on earth. The energy in my body accelerated at a frantic rate; it seemed extremely angry and violent, and I often thought it would blow me off the road we were walking on. That I was struggling to hold it together was apparent to those around me, and it was torture knowing that, after several weeks of this, I wasn't any closer to understanding what was going on with me.

I had been planning a trip to Las Vegas to work with one of my recovery mentors; we were hoping to get some clarity about my situation. With only a week to go before I got on the plane, I was very fearful about flying to Las Vegas alone in my condition. But I was really counting on the upcoming work in Vegas to create a shift in my circumstances, or even to resolve my situation completely.

I never anticipated what would happen during the week leading up to the Vegas trip.

I was still getting virtually no sleep and was exhausted all the time. I particularly dreaded the nighttime because it meant being alone, and I was having terrible night terrors. I would lie in the dark room—my thoughts racing, the coursing energy having its way with me—and I would wonder whether or not I would still be alive in the morning; whether the coming day would be the one that forced me to check myself into a hospital; whether I would ever find the road map that would lead me back to my life the way it used to be.

To prepare for bed, I would take some melatonin, a hormone-based sleep aid, and drink some chamomile tea, which is an herbal tea that is very calming and can also help induce sleep. Yet despite these steps, I was able to fall asleep for only minutes at a time. It was a bit like that scene from *Groundhog Day*. Over and over I would awaken to see the red digits on my alarm clock, then I'd realize I had been asleep for only minutes, not hours. It was a horrible feeling because I knew what lay ahead of me for the rest of the night.

Intense, unbearable waves of heat would take over my body, only to be replaced by the sensation of a cold energy passing through me, forcing me to wrap myself tightly in the bedding to warm up. As I lay there with my eyes closed, on the back of my eyelids I would observe an elaborate display of light. Then, by some grace, I would steal thirty minutes of sleep, only to be awakened by a strange sound or a vision. I would hear water rushing over a waterfall, lions roaring, the wind howling, bees humming, and/or the ocean crashing against rocks. I sometimes saw people in my visions—people who were really important to me. Other times I saw faces and people I didn't know and I would get a strong impression that I was visiting past lifetimes. At times I would be convinced that snakes, large and small, were in the bed with me. Burying my head under my pillow offered no escape. The forks of lightening shooting across my mind's eye and around my head continued to pursue me.

I prayed to God for the madness to stop. On occasion I would cry out and ask Him what I had done to deserve this; I'd plead to be left alone and to be granted mercy. Eventually, the sun would rise, and another day would begin—a day of confusion and struggle—a day that I had nonetheless prayed for all night. But within hours, that day would become so painful and lonely that again I would pray for night to come around, at which point I would restlessly toss and turn and try to quiet my racing mind. There seemed to be no way out of this cycle I was trapped in.

Then it happened: One evening the friends I was staying with asked if I wanted to watch a movie to try to take my mind off things. I agreed. As I sat there trying, without much success, to focus on the TV screen, I felt a ball of energy gather at the base of my spine, just above my pelvic area. When I looked down, I could see lights flashing in my body, as if a fireworks display was taking place within me. Bright blue lights seemed to intertwine and coil around a very dark entity, which looked like a dragon or a dark serpent. The dark entity appeared to be fighting the light. The two forces twisted and tangled and circled around each other, like tinsel wrapping around a Christmas tree and every bit as colorful. As they made their way up my spine, I watched with amazement as this scene played out. I could scarcely believe what was happening. On some level, it felt as if a battle for my very soul was taking place.

Eventually, this ball of twisting coiling energy rushed up my spine and exploded right through my brain and my crown chakra with a burst of blue-and-gold colored lights. As this happened, I was nearly blown out of my chair. The entire experience had been both unbelievable and breathtaking. I sat, stunned, for a few moments, trying to process what had just happened, and a feeling of utter peace washed over me. I thoroughly welcomed the sensation. Then I walked into the kitchen and tried to explain to my friend what had just occurred. She hugged me and said she hoped I was going to be okay.

It seemed to me that something major had just taken place. I didn't know what it was, but I was sure it would prove to be a major turning point and that peace would be with me from there on out because freedom from my intense dilemma had finally shown up. However, while this was undoubtedly true, and while I did feel a sense of peace, the peace was not to last.

I had just felt the Kundalini—the Divine—God's hand on my shoulder. That is what, through my struggles, I had been pushing away. I had, at times in my life, asked to be closer to God when I found myself locked in dark struggles. Well, apparently "God" had arrived, but not in the package I was expecting.

My assumption, based on the views of people I respected and books I had read, was that the Divine, and its arrival, would be blissful. Of course, the Divine *can* show up that way—God can make an appearance in an infinite number of ways. But the more evolved people I have spoken to since, agree that not all awakenings are pleasant, especially if, like me, you haven't got a clue what's actually going on. I wasn't to understand for a few years what was happening to me, and those years would be hell—sheer hell—at times. I often thought it was like being on a bad LSD trip from which I just couldn't come down. I wish I had understood then what was taking place, but I recognize now that I had to experience this awakening just the way it occurred.

That fireworks display, or ball of energy, that I had observed moving up my spine had been, I was to learn years later, a depiction of the symbol of Kundalini—a serpent coiled around a staff. We see it often in today's society, and most people don't really give it a second thought or a glance. It's the symbol for medicine that's used in the United States and it's called the "caduceus."

I would learn more about the caduceus a few years later when I was attending a Kundalini seminar in upstate New York. Our assembled group was discussing the different experiences each of us had had. Listening to the others, I realized that what had occurred to me in Pennsylvania was that my Kundalini had awakened, which was followed by the spinal sweep. Looking back I would say that the Kundalini energy had already activated in my body; the spinal sweep was an experience within the Kundalini awakening experience. I was also later to find out that not everyone with activated Kundalini has the spinal sweep experience; things differ from person to person. (Sometimes the ego likes to use an experience to make itself seem grandiose. Other times, such as in this case, it has a very powerful way of downplaying an experience and convincing me that something I'd gone through was simply inconsequential.)

* * *

In any event, the real fun was about to begin. About a week later I was back in Pennsylvania at my friends' house, and I was feeling nervous about my upcoming trip to Las Vegas. To prepare for my meeting, I had been speaking to my mentor from the recovery community—the very guy I was going to meet in Vegas—trying to explain my predicament to him, but without much success. Talk about feeling misunderstood!

Additionally, I hadn't known him for that long so he probably thought I was nuts. It seemed to everyone that I had maybe veered off track a little and simply needed to work the recovery program a bit to regain my equilibrium. Actually, on some level, I was hoping and praying that they were right and that my doing some additional work would be all it took to get my life back again. If more recovery work was needed, I would at least have a familiar reference point from which to start. But deep down I knew it wasn't going to be that easy.

Looking back, all I can do is laugh when I remember how I actually tried to verbalize to people what I was experiencing. I can only imagine what was going through their minds as I tried to paint as vivid a picture as I could for them. At the time, though, I wasn't laughing. Being totally misunderstood by many people, frequently written off as crazy, and repeatedly told I was just self-centered and needed to get my shit together was frustrating as hell. I guess when someone thinks they know everything about a particular subject, they have to say what they feel is right, especially when they're working from a finite point of view. Even today many of those same people still think I just went a little crazy for a time. When the contents of your life are being dragged up and pulled to the surface at an alarming speed, you will certainly appear to be crazy.

What I have come to know is that what I was going through was a completely natural aspect of a real awakening process, which seems crazy to most people because they never get to experience that. Be that as it may, I did need all those people in my life at that time to play their parts. Although they couldn't really help me get to the bottom of my problem, they did help keep me alive until I could do that for myself.

Life was almost unbearable for, as mentioned earlier, I was living with the constant fear that I would have to resort to drinking or using drugs, and the energy coursing through my body felt like a nonstop attack. In retrospect, I imagine it felt like a possession, although at the time I never seriously had the notion that a demon had overtaken my body, even though it felt like I was doing battle with demons every day. I had developed an extreme sensitivity to both sunlight and touch, which reinforced my concerns that I might be nuts.

* * *

As the day of the flight grew closer, I realized that I was pinning all my hopes on this man in Las Vegas, who I knew had helped many others. I had to believe that he would do something extraordinary for me, too.

I'll never forget that challenging flight and the layover in Chicago's O'Hare Airport. It was probably the worst trip of my life to date, but was nothing compared to what was in store for me over the next few months. I remember finally touching down in Las Vegas and the kind man who was waiting for me, taking time out of his life to pick me up. Bob was a great man who had probably helped more people than anyone else I knew. He had a lot of wisdom and a unique way of getting to the bottom of things, using the bag of skillful tricks he possessed. We immediately stopped for an afternoon meeting, then had lunch and went back to his house in the desert, where we talked for hours as he tried to coax out of me what was going on. I did feel somewhat safe in his company and at his home, but there was clearly something not right with me and the fear of drinking and/or doing drugs was still very present. I felt like a high-maintenance kid who everyone was trying to fix, and the vibe I was getting from the others was "just do what we do and you'll be fine," which couldn't have been further from the truth.

When I was able to think clearly, I recognized that I had made great progress in my recovery work for a decade. I had done some really deep work; anyone who knew me would vouch for this. My whole life had changed as a result of my efforts. I was a true advocate of recovery and how to go about it. I'd had some excellent teachers and was sincerely grateful to all who had played a role in liberating me from drinking and in guiding me to a much better life.

Sometimes my recovery work had also brought up a lot of suffering, and when that happened, I struggled to understand why—when I was focusing so hard on working the program— at times I just seemed in the dark. I knew that with recovery came growing pains, but the suffering I'm talking about seemed to far exceed the norm, sometimes to the point of brutality. Long before this mysterious energy hijacked my body, I recall going into dark spiritual depressions and getting stuck there without any real explanations for any of it. I remember times when the cycles of anxiety and fear seemed like they would never leave me alone, almost to the point that it seemed like I was haunted. I went through a traumatic episode in 2007 that brought me to the brink of insanity. I was a decent guy, not misbehaving in any way at all trying to live a life with good ethics and morality, who was trying to help people, and so I couldn't figure out why my suffering seemed so out of proportion.

It seemed like I was sick, but then again it didn't seem like a sickness at all. What I mean to say is that stuff from my past would rise into my awareness as though it wanted to exit my system. It felt like I was reliving old traumatic events from my present life and sometimes previous lives. At times this sensation would hit me all at once and be almost unbearable and I would find it impossible to function in a normal way. I suppose in my naiveté I was convinced I should have known what the spiritual journey should actually look like. This wasn't the way it was supposed to be going. How foolish of me to think this!

As mentioned earlier, at this time I did reach out to various teachers and mentors of mine from the 12-step program, however, I was very selective about who I approached for help. If I had fully opened up and really shared what was going on with me in recovery circles, my words would have freaked out practically everyone. Thus, I knew instinctively not to do that, even though I *desperately* wanted to find a person, whoever it might be, that would have some answers for me.

In Las Vegas with my mentor, I did share specific details about what I was going through. His response, however, was that I should just keep doing what I was doing: sticking close to the program and practicing the things that I had been doing that had gotten me this far. He also told me he didn't know whether or not I would be okay, and in this, he was just being as honest as he could with me.

We did our work, but my circumstances didn't change at all. I remember lying on his sofa, feeling that cold energy rip through my body and the lightning crack around my head. My whole being seemed to vibrate with a continuous humming sound. I couldn't sit in a chair for more than two minutes at a time, so I paced endlessly around his house. I pleaded with God to have mercy on my soul. I wanted to cry because I was afraid for my life, but something within wouldn't even allow me to produce the tears. I lay huddled under the blanket, or paced frantically from room to room. There is only so much a man can take, and I didn't know where that line was. If the energy had been turned up by one notch it would have killed me for sure. I think my heart and my head might have exploded.

I grew to understand, however, that I'm one of the strongest, most strong willed people I know. It took everything in me, mentally and emotionally, to keep going under these conditions. Everything I had learned—about life, about spiritual practice, about sheer survival—just went right out the window as I was forced to totally surrender. (We all like to think we're in control; but what are we really in control of?) Like many, I used to enjoy that sense of power, that feeling that I was living life by my terms, that I was really *doing it*. But this process, which had me in its grip, was showing me that I wasn't in control, that being in control was simply a delusional idea.

What kept me going more than anything else was the love I have for my family, especially my daughter, Fianna, who I love more than words can express. That love was a super motivator that propelled me toward whatever help I could find. I was about to learn what it's like to fight for my life, to survive until tomorrow because of a tremendous will to live another day. When it seems as if life may be taken from you at any moment, an amazing will to live springs up. I can only imagine what it would be like to be diagnosed with a terminal illness and given a window of time in which to live. I suspect that my impulse to fight, to give it everything I had, was similar to the reaction of many who are newly diagnosed with a terminal illness.

In short, I was about to see what this Irishman was really made of.

I had a long talk with my mentor; it lasted nearly five hours. We sat in the living room in his rather modern villa going step by step through a process that is sometimes used in recovery circles to identify stuff that needs to be cleared up. I was eager to tackle that clearing right away. But despite the work that my mentor and I were doing, my fears surrounding the obsession to drink booze and use drugs was getting stronger and my inner condition seemed to become more frantic by the minute. This simply didn't add up! From what I was aware of people who apply the techniques I was working with, who go to the depths I was going, generally do not experience a *strengthening* of their obsession. I had never heard of this happening and when I told my mentor what was going on, he looked shocked. I imagine he had never heard of this happening either. I didn't know it at the time, but working the recovery practices in the condition I was in was like trying to put out a blazing forest fire with a watering can.

I would see later on that the work I did with my mentor during those days together played a part in grounding me and helping me in many other ways, but it did not address the extraordinary circumstances I found myself in. What I was going through had nothing to do with my alcoholism or my recovery, and the language of the 12 steps would never get me to the bottom of what was going on. And that's what I so desperately needed to know: *What is happening to me?* It was certainly something quite extreme, but I couldn't effectively describe my condition to anyone, and I had yet to find anyone who could help me uncover the answers that I so desperately needed.

My mentor and I went to a conference in San Antonio the next day. I remember sitting in the Las Vegas airport feeling distressed and disappointed that my predicament had not improved and, if anything, was getting worse. The energy was ripping and roaring and really letting me know it was there. The freaky thoughts that were shooting through my mind were creating utter turmoil within my entire system.

We stayed in a beautiful hotel right beside the very picturesque river walk in San Antonio, just ten minutes from the Alamo. There I was seeing firsthand some of the coolest sites America had to offer, but I wasn't enjoying my stay at all. Instead, I remember walking along the very artsy Americana sidewalks alone, feeling at an all-time low—petrified, anxious, afraid for my life—and unable to communicate my condition to anyone. I was thinking that perhaps I was some freak of nature who wouldn't find a way through this. Furthermore, I was not looking forward to going back to New York City, to an empty apartment, without having found some sort of answer. That thought disturbed me deeply, especially because I had no good ideas about where to turn next. I was gravely concerned about what the future held for me.

I wasn't to get to the bottom of anything for quite some time, and there was still a lot of pain, suffering, frustration, self-pity, and despair for me to go through. However, I could see that the universe was trying to provide for me. At least, I wanted very badly to believe that, for it was all I had to pin my hopes on at that point, so I used that as an auspice. I was trying to focus on the positives: I had a place to live, and people in my life who regularly showed up to help me. Additionally, small strokes of luck were arriving out of the blue every day, sometimes just enough to keep me going.

* * *

Back in New York it was more of the same: I was freaked out about what the hell was happening, and I had to have long telephone calls with people just to stay sane. Sometimes I would go into a shaking and jerking frenzy. There was no relief whatsoever. It's no wonder people thought I sounded crazy at times. Regrettably, Western medicine is so far behind the times when it comes to treating spiritual emergencies.

I continued to travel back and forth to my friends' home in Pennsylvania as the summer months arrived. We sat in back of their house and watched the kids play in their pool, and we'd have long discussions about everything we had each gone through that had brought us to where we were and that brought some comfort.

Even with all the recovery work and spiritual fellowship I was doing, I just wasn't getting to the bottom of anything. The fear that the obsession to drink alcohol would return to my life plagued me, as well as the terror that I might be driven to shoot heroin just to numb what was happening. The fact I had never had any desire to try heroin in the past was irrelevant; the idea still kept popping into my head to torment me and that was extremely disturbing.

Obsession is a very strange and frightening ordeal; in my case, the fear of the return of my obsession rapped on my door hour after hour, day after day, month after month. Though taking a drink might not sound like a big deal to people who don't understand the mechanism that drives alcoholism and other addictions, a drink is, in fact, a *very* big deal. For me, to drink is to die, and that probably means a slow death as an alcoholic. The scariest aspects of drinking are the consequences: the guilt, the shame, the remorse, the unbearable darkness. I feared the anger, the self-loathing, the potential hospital visits, the thoughts of suicide, the loss of my apartment, the loss of my job, and the respect I would lose from the people I knew—among other things. (An alcoholic in recovery will understand exactly what I mean.)

My eight-year-old daughter had never seen me drunk. In her innocence, she didn't even know the person I used to be, and the thought of my becoming that person again scared the hell out of me. I worried, too, that I would run out of money. I had a little breathing space—some savings —but I knew I could never function as an ironworker on a high-rise building in my condition. So I was genuinely afraid that I would end up homeless, on the street, and not able to take care of myself. (Later on, I met people who had undergone experiences similar to mine, and they *did* end up living on the street. One gentleman in particular who I became very friendly with had been homeless in California for more than ten years—a brutal existence for anyone to endure.)

One of the manifestations of my condition was that everything I could see, feel, think, or experience in any way was amplified—turned up to the absolute max. This resulted in a super sensitivity to nearly everything. One of the hardest parts of my whole experience was the isolation I felt as a result of my not being able to communicate successfully what was occurring within me. And when I *did* try to share what was happening, I often felt strangely violated. Over and over I would reveal details about what I was experiencing in the hope of finding some type of help, but more often than not I was met with wary expressions, confused looks, and startled faces. I soon learned to become much more careful in whom I chose to confide.

Living in Western society with this mystery condition was never easy, especially when I was in father mode and spending time with my daughter. Fianna is a very special person and a very wise soul; she knew something wasn't right with her dad and really tried to help me in her own little ways, which was amazing, given her young age. Fianna was very understanding and her behavior when she was with me was unbelievable. I really tried to hold it together as best I could when we were together.

Chapter 3
Introducing the Irish "Horse Whisperer"

Around Easter of 2011 I had decided to schedule a holiday in Ocean City, Maryland, for the Fourth of July weekend. I'd been wanting to take Fianna to the beach, and my sister Kathy was coming to visit from London. I thought it would be a great idea to get both of them out of the city heat and treat them to some seaside sun. So I booked a nice condo by the beach in Ocean City—no place like the ocean for the Fourth of July! Normally, I would have been psyched about such a trip and excited to spend time with my family, but by the time the trip rolled around, I just wasn't feeling it at all—quite the opposite, actually.

God works in mysterious ways, and I was about to get real firsthand knowledge of this as the universe began throwing lifesavers my way, one by one, in an amazing pattern: An obstacle or problem would appear, and with it all the related fear, stress, and suffering. These emotions would then be cranked up by what seemed to be an amplifier, so much so that everything my mind threw at me seemed fifty times worse than it really was, and it would all bash me continuously. I had no way of determining with any kind of accuracy the actual magnitude of what was taking place—it *all* seemed so real. Then I would reach out to ask for guidance in the midst of the struggle, and something would happen as if an answer to my prayers. God was showing me He had my back, but with everything I was going through, believing God was with me was really rough. It seemed like my faith, along with my mind, had to be reborn over and over again.

Much to my surprise, my sister was one of the first lifesavers that the universe tossed out to me. I expected help to come in the form of a spiritual book or a wise teacher, but no, it came by way of Kathy, so I wasn't prepared or even all that receptive to what was about to take place. Kathy was closest to me in the family packing order, being four years older than me. I suppose

I'd spent more time with her over the years than I had with the rest of my siblings. She'd had success as an actress and had moved to London to pursue her career when she was young and had lived between there and Ireland ever since. It had paid off for her as she had landed many parts in different films and shows over the years; she had even starred in her own TV series back in Belfast. Having her with me was comforting, but I didn't grasp the impact that her presence would ultimately have on my story.

I picked Kathy up at the airport in Newark and it didn't take my sister very long to figure out that something was wrong with me. Kathy and I had grown up together in the same house, after all, and she knew me pretty well. She had witnessed my dark days of alcoholism; now she recognized that I was borderline out of my mind. This was despite the fact that I was trying to pull off the strong-man routine and pretend that everything was fine. During the drive from Newark to Queens, we stuck to small talk because Fianna was in the car, but I could tell Kathy was anxious to speak to me one-on-one.

When we got back to my apartment, Fianna was distracted watching TV and Kathy and I finally got a chance to have a candid conversation. She was clearly alarmed when I shared what was going on with me; I could see that concern written all over her face and in every gesture from there on out. Having Kathy come and stay with us felt really great—I very much welcomed the company —but my fears were still alarming. I kept hitting what seemed like one new hopeless low point after another, and that's what happened the day we drove from New York City to Ocean City, Maryland, too. The five-hour-plus drive was not so bad; listening to music in the car and stopping for lunch distracted me quite a bit. But once we arrived at our condo and settled in, I was overtaken by an abject feeling of despair. It was impossible for me to remain strong and focus on creating a joyous holiday, and there came a point when I just couldn't pretend anymore. I fell right to pieces.

It happened during dinner in a restaurant: the energy exploded through my body, followed by an orchestra of thunder that sent bright lights flashing through my head. In a panic, I jumped up from the table and ran outside. I could see my sister's eyes grow wide as she took in my behavior and tried to keep Fianna occupied so she wouldn't be upset by my disappearance.

I didn't know what the fuck to do and had never been so helpless in all my life. It felt as if my sanity could slip away from me at any moment, and the fear that this could actually happen––that I could lose my mind forever—tormented me. All of those fears would feed off one another, and my ego would create story after story that would race through my mind at an alarming rate. When the ego has no frame of reference to work from, it goes into panic mode. And my system had gone into shock, which prohibited me from functioning properly. One more time my ego scanned the filing cabinets of my belief system, just to see if there was a piece of information somewhere that it could hold onto—one thing it could use to generate a sliver of control. However, the ego wasn't coming up with any matches for my current series of events.

The basic function of the ego is to serve. Without it, I would have to learn how to drive my car every time I got into it or I might not know what time I needed to be at the airport for an upcoming flight. I do need my ego for a lot of things, but I don't need it to figure out my future or my destiny. And this was a major cause of suffering for me: my ego constantly brought me out of a present moment to worry about the future or the past.

I didn't know what my next step was going to be as I ran out of the restaurant that evening. Again, when we got back to the condo, I was on the phone with friends, trying to explain what I was enduring and seeking advice about what to do. But I felt bad for my sister, who had travelled so far just to watch me freak out.

Kathy, however, really pitched in. She rolled her sleeves up and started to take care of Fianna and me. She tried to help me get to the bottom of what was happening, and we sat and talked for hours. Sometimes our conversations became emotional or heated; sometimes we argued—no, even yelled—at each other (of course, we'd been doing that since we were kids!). We had no problem speaking our minds, which really was a great blessing at this time.

One evening we were sitting on the balcony of the condo, talking and listening to the ocean. Kathy began to tell me about her best friend's family who had recently bought a new house, but they weren't happy with it—there were rather some strange things going-on there. Someone had suggested that the friend consult a guy named Trevor, who was a "Horse Whisperer" and seemed to have other special gifts as well, which I understood to be psychic abilities. I was often skeptical of these claims; in fact, I guess you could say I was closed-minded. In any event, Kathy said that Trevor knew how to remove dark energies from people and places, and my sister's friend had invited Trevor to the new home.

The night that Trevor visited the house, which was located in the north of Ireland, my sister and some other friends had been invited to attend, too. Kathy went on to say that Trevor had examined the house from top to bottom, then explained to everyone that the disruptive problem was due to the fact that there was a restless soul on the premises—someone who had been killed years previously. Trevor said that he was going to guide this lost soul to the other side, and apparently, he walked it right through the back door and out of the house, never to return. Kathy said Trevor could detect entities in people, too, and that he had done some other work in this area in addition to the house cleanse.

Honestly, all this talk of ghosts and entities just freaked me out, and I let Kathy know it in no uncertain terms. Yet she hit back, calling me a know-it-all, and we argued for a bit. I couldn't see how what she was telling me had any connection at all to my situation. I was totally pissed and didn't want to hear another word about any of it.

Those days in Ocean City were challenging, to say the least, even though it was lovely to have time with Fianna and Kathy. I didn't know it then, but hanging out in the sunlight was one of the last things I should have been doing in my condition. I was super sensitive to sunlight, physical touch, and other people's energy because my chakras—the body's energy centers—were wide open and. Over the next days, I was to gain a better understanding of this.

* * *

As time went on I began to realize that I could feel other people's energy in a deep way. This was unlike anything I had ever experienced before. I had no filter and didn't know how to shake the accrued energy off of me. Unwittingly taking on someone else's dark or heavy energy would exhaust me for hours. It wouldn't be until years later that I would learn how to release such energies and to protect myself by putting up boundaries to prevent me from taking them on in the first place.

It was difficult living in a city like New York and being as spiritually open as I was at that point in time. For example, when I rode the subway, I would take on the energies of the other passengers around me, and I felt as if I was actually living out their emotions and energies with them. Or if I was reading a newspaper story about a child or someone who was being raped, harmed, or abused in any way, I would be instantly sad—sometimes to the point of tears. When I saw homeless people on the street, I would take on the distress they felt about their situation and would be compelled to give them money or find some other way to help them.

Reading other people's energy is known as "clairvoyance" in spiritual circles, but at the time I didn't have a clue why negative energy would hijack my system and hitch a ride. I *did* know, however, that these energies were often very tricky to deal with, especially the ones I picked up at recovery-based meetings. In general, addicts and alcoholics carry around some very dark vibes. So operating from this level was all new ground for me, and it was quite amazing. Yet it was plain to see that no one else around me was operating in this way, not that I was aware of, anyway. I would eventually meet people who were open to all these energies, and who knew how to manage them far more successfully than I did.

At the time, I had no way of grounding the energies or filtering them like I can today, after having been taught to do so by skilled teachers and healers. I have since learned that whatever I allow to enter through the front door, I must invite to exit through the back, or I pay a heavy price.

* * *

The next step along my path to healing came through an old friend who I had not spoken to for quite a while, ever since we'd had a falling-out. I had known Barefoot Bill for more than five years, and he probably knew me as well as anyone at that time. Some friends suggested I reach out to him and let him know what was going on with me. I didn't really want to do that because things had ended badly between us, and the last time I had spoken to him I had really let him have a piece of my mind. But I had reached a new low point, and in weighing my options, I realized I simply had nowhere else to turn. Barefoot Bill was a spiritual, hippie sort of character who would sometimes wear pajama pants with penguins on them coupled with tie-dyed shirts. I had met him years previously at a conference in New York. He was definitely a unique character who became a spiritual guide for me after I'd had some conversations with him about meditation. He had a major interest and involvement in the spiritual world and introduced me to books and people that no one in my circles seemed to have heard of. I had done quite a bit of in-depth work with Bill so it was safe to say he knew me fairly well. He was a good dude who'd really helped me a lot at one particular time in my life.

I was really thinking that God had abandoned me and I wasn't going to make it out of my predicament alive. Doing the things that had been part of my program for a decade—praying and helping others go to meetings, for instance—offered me no hope or relief. And I couldn't meditate anymore because the energy coursing through my body, along with all the other turmoil, wouldn't let me sit still for more than a few seconds. So I did end up reaching out to my old friend Bill, and I remember just crying out on the phone when he picked up.

He quickly asked me what was wrong, and I could hear the alarm in his voice. I was talking a million miles an hour, just spitting out everything that had been going on. My friend seemed a bit shocked by my manner, but I could tell he was happy to hear from me and that he was also concerned about my state. I went through the whole story with him, and he listened to me carefully for nearly two hours, asking several questions. Finally, he asked me whether I had been behaving myself in my life, or whether I had been misbehaving myself in any way—just simple questions using the process of elimination. I had never been a saint, and he knew that, but I was totally honest with him and told him that I had been doing really well before all this had started, and he believed me.

Bill said that he didn't want to freak me out, but he was going to give me his opinion, using biblical terms, about what might be wrong with me. I was cool with that as he wasn't a religious man and he knew I wasn't either. Then he said that he thought perhaps I was possessed. Well, never in a million years would I have even considered that a possibility, and I was gob smacked. I was also very grateful to him for his honest evaluation, and I trusted him because he knew me so well. His words threw a different spin on things, and while they didn't change my dilemma, they did remind me how much my recovery program had given me and how I totally did not want to lose all the ground I'd gained in the 12-step work I'd done. I had to find a way to move beyond my constant obsession that booze and/or drugs would once again take me over.

I'd had a deep-seated belief from the beginning of my experience that what I was experiencing was outside the scope of the spiritual practices I typically relied on, and outside of what the people in my recovery circles knew. I also understood that, on some level, I needed help beyond what was available from my 12-step program. The cofounder of the program had once said that the program was a spiritual kindergarten, and I was finding out the truth of those words the hard way. Very soon I would be introduced to people and activities that made everything I had experienced up to that point seem like I had been playing in the sandpit at that kindergarten.

It was my friend Bill's girlfriend's birthday, and a bunch of us were getting together at a restaurant in New Jersey to celebrate. My friend had asked me to stop off at his place of business before we went to the restaurant. I'd not seen him for months––I had only spoken to him on the phone––so when I arrived at his high-end furniture showroom, he could see how distressed I was. He remarked that he knew I wasn't doing well from our phone calls, but he hadn't realized I was so bad off.

Dinner was extremely difficult for me—the amount of energy crashing through my body during social situations was all but unbearable. I sat beside my friend and reviewed my story with him in some detail. Just by chance, I mentioned to him that Kathy and Fianna and I had gone to Ocean City on vacation and, while there, Kathy had told me the strange story about Trevor the Horse Whisperer. Without hesitation, Bill encouraged me to go see Trevor as soon as possible. He told me straight out that I had to find Trevor right away. When I hesitated, he asked if I had any better ideas.

I'll never forget the distress I felt standing outside that restaurant in the middle of New Jersey—just wishing at that point that it would all just end. I looked at Bill in that parking lot in an absolute terror and asked, "Where is God in all this?" He said not to worry, that God was right there with me. As much as I wanted to believe him, I was skeptical that God could be connected in any way to the mess I was in.

Back then my beliefs about God were very warped and finite. Even today I try not to use the word *God*, because it doesn't seem to do justice to the power that exists and is present in the universe. I had been in many bleak tunnels in my life, including during my sobriety when I sometimes found myself in spiritual deserts, which I recall as being very dark. I had often dealt with very bad depression, and had been nearly driven over the edge by it many times.

One strange part about my current situation, however, was that I wasn't depressed—not at all. Any time I've ever run into trouble in the past, depression would show up as well. If this condition I was experiencing had been joined by depression, it certainly would have been "lights out" for me.

That night I stayed with a friend in New Jersey, and we sat up until the small hours talking; she was very kind and offered to let me stay in her house for as long as I wished. Over and over, I encountered that type of generosity from people I've met on the spiritual path, especially in the United States. Some folks were just so willing to go above and beyond to help me.

That night in my friend's house was a very rough one, indeed. The voices within me were just relentless: "Get high, get drunk, run away from it all, sign yourself in somewhere," and on and on. Although I'd been hearing them for a few months now, they continued to grow louder and louder. More than ever I feared for my sanity. That night the energy surging within me was so forceful I felt myself being forcefully moved around on the bed.

Years of pain, suffering, a deep depression, and a suicide attempt had brought me into the rooms of recovery the first time, when I was desperate for a way out. That had been back in Ireland when I was a young man. Actually, I'd been in and out of the rooms of recovery for a few years back in Ireland before I eventually did get sober. Now I once again needed a way out, but this time it wasn't through booze or drugs. I was seriously considering the possibility that a demon had me by the tail and was refusing to let go.

I got up early the next morning and sent my sister an email explaining that I'd had a change of heart and would like to be put in contact with Trevor, if at all possible. She acted quickly; within an hour she had his phone number for me. As I drove the New Jersey Turnpike back toward New York City later that day, with the Manhattan skyline just coming into view, I dialed Trevor's number in Ireland.

When a mild-sounding Ulster voice answered on the other end and said that yes, he was Trevor, I explained to him who I was. He asked how I had gotten his number, and I mentioned the names of the people Kathy had told me about. Then he asked me in a very kind voice what was going on with me, and I started to explain my situation to him. He indicated that he could sense that I wasn't doing well and that I hadn't been for some months. And he said that, if I was interested, he would see me.

I explained to him that I was in New York City, and he asked if I would be coming to Ireland anytime soon. I told him that depended on whether he thought he could help me. He said he thought he could, then he explained that, the way he worked, he needed to be able to put his hands on me. When I asked him why, he replied that, based on our conversation on the phone, he could tell I was possessed. He was able to hear whatever it was that was in me. I was shocked but not at all surprised given that my sister and friend Bill had already nailed it, and I was becoming more willing to believe it with each passing day. I asked him with desperation whether he could definitely help me if I made the trip to Belfast, and he repeated that he could—this was his professional work and he had helped many others before me.

I didn't know whether to laugh or cry, but I had to believe he was genuine. We began talking about what I did in New York, and he struck me as a friendly, sincere fellow. I told him that as soon as I hung up the phone, I would find the next available flight to Ireland. He said he would come to Belfast and meet me on Thursday, and he asked what part of Belfast I was from.

When I told him I was from Andersonstown in West Belfast, he said we should meet somewhere else. I later realized why he didn't want to go to West Belfast: Trevor was an ex-RUC (Royal Ulster Constabulary) man. The RUC was the British police force that had been involved in the conflict between the Catholics and the Protestants, upholding the Protestants' desire to remain British during the years I was growing up. Let's just say members of the RUC "weren't on my team." I had taken a beating from them, been arrested by them, been victimized, brutalized . . . A long history of run-ins with the RUC had left indelible marks on my psyche, including being shot on the leg by them with a plastic bullet at the scene of a riot in North Belfast when I was younger.

I asked Trevor repeatedly whether he could really help me, and he assured me over and over again that he could. Overcome by fear and agony, I asked him if I would be okay; whether I would make it until I saw him that Thursday. He said that I would. Trevor's confirmation that I was possessed—by someone who had experience in this realm—frightened me profoundly. However, along with the freak-out came a slight sense of relief. I had been running on empty for quite a while, and I knew in my heart that the time was rapidly approaching when I would no longer be able to keep going without some serious help.

I had told Trevor that I was in hell and really needed our work together to be successful. I went on to ask him if there was anything I could do to make this dark energy retreat a bit until I could see him that Thursday. He told me to recite the Lord's Prayer over and over, no matter whether I considered myself a Christian or not. He explained that the words *deliver us from evil* would help hold off any evil energies within me. He also told me that when I met with him in Belfast, I should have a piece of gold in my pocket. A small piece of it would do, but it had to be real gold for our work together to be effective. I asked him if there was anything I could bring him from the States for helping me. He thought for a few seconds and replied that he'd like a good bottle of American bourbon. I pointed out that it disturbed me a little bit that he would ask me to bring him alcohol, considering the condition I was in. He agreed, and then said that I should just bring myself.

As I completed my drive back to Queens I continued to review every word that Trevor and I had exchanged during our phone chat. I was *possessed*. That made sense to me, but I wondered how it could have happened. I didn't know anything about possession at all. My only exposure to it had been by watching some really freaky movies over the years. In fact, I had never watched them through to the end because I had been so freaked out by them.

I got back to my apartment, logged onto my computer, and immediately started looking for a flight to Belfast. I found a seat available on the 10:00 p.m. flight that Tuesday night. The plane would land at Belfast International Airport, which is only about twenty-five minutes from my parents' house. Even though the ticket cost me over fifteen hundred dollars, I bought it, for money was the least of my concerns at that point. Had the flight cost me twenty grand and required me to take out a loan to finance it, I would gladly have done so.

That night I met my brother Mark and explained to him what I was going through. I also told him that, according to Trevor, I was clinically possessed. Mark was my older brother, ten years older to be exact, and second oldest out of my siblings. We'd been pretty close when I first came to the States but had taken different paths as time went on. Still in all, he would have done anything for me. I explained that I would be flying home to Belfast in a few days to meet a horse whisperer who was going to perform an exorcism on me. Upset, Mark asked how such a thing as being possessed could have happened to me. I told him I had no idea, and that I was concerned about what I was going to tell our parents and sisters as to why I was coming home on such short notice. He told me that he would call them in advance and explain things as best he could.

The next morning my phone rang and rang. My sisters and my father were calling from Ireland to check in with me. I knew my brother had, true to his word, called them to fill them in on what was taking place. (My mom, it seems, had suspected something was up because over the past several months I had not been calling home as regularly as I normally did.)

Even though I didn't want to deal with anyone, I called my father back; I knew he would keep calling me until I picked up. The conversation didn't go as I wanted it to, but it did go as I expected. He went on about how I should go back to church and start attending mass on Sundays; how I should never have stepped away from my faith. I understood he was concerned and afraid for me and was only reacting the way a frightened father would, so I just let him ramble on. Although my father does go to church every week, he is far from what you would call religious, and he's definitely not into spirituality. But he is a very kind and loving man, one from whom great energy and a lot of light emanate. I think those attributes are more important than anything else, so I let him have his say. And although I didn't like all the fuss and drama from my family one bit, in a way I was glad they knew what I'd been going through because it saved me from having to explain things when I got back to Belfast. I believed it was a good thing that my family lived so far away and hadn't seen what had been going on: that would have been scary for them to watch.

The flight was a few days away, so I began to get my travel arrangements in order. I wasn't a gold jewelry type of guy, thus I didn't have the piece of gold I needed. I went to a store not far from my apartment to see what was available. Ideally, I wanted something small and inexpensive. Unfortunately, the price of gold was quite high, and the smallest thing they had was a pair of gold earrings. I didn't want those. Seeing a rather attractive gold cross, I asked the salesman if it was real gold. He confirmed that it was, and so for nearly three hundred dollars, I bought the cross.

My next errand was to go to the bank for some cash and travelers checks, but whatever the hell was inside me was letting me know, in no uncertain terms, that it was now *completely* crazy. My mind was racing like it never had before; the energies were ripping through my being; the voices were clamoring; it was full-scale mayhem, and I truly felt as if I was about to explode. I don't know which was more difficult—dealing with the actual attack I seemed to be under or acting normal in front of people while I was under attack. I recall having to run out of the Chase bank on Woodside Avenue in Queens because the energy that was flooding my system was so great I couldn't take it anymore.

Like a madman, I sprinted across the street and right onto the steps of the rectory of St. Sebastian's Church. I pressed frantically on the buzzer, and eventually an older lady's voice came through the speaker on the door. I told her I needed a priest immediately. When she asked why, I begged her just to get the priest and not ask why. I added that she really didn't want to know. She opened the door, ushered me inside, took me into a little room and went to fetch the priest. After a few minutes, a middle-aged man in priest's attire entered. He introduced himself as a monsignor and asked the reason for my visit.

I told him I thought I was possessed, then watched his whole demeanor change. He seemed a little bit flustered yet definitely interested in what I had to say. He listened intently as my story spilled out, not being able to hide the fact that he was disturbed by it all. I told him everything, including my plans to fly to Ireland to meet with a horse whisperer who was going to try to help me.

The monsignor was in total agreement with my plan. It was pretty clear he didn't know what else to do, for he definitely didn't have the skills himself to remove whatever was inside of me. I hadn't expected him to. I was just grateful that he had come to talk to me. He excused himself and left the room briefly, then returned with a container of something—it seemed like some kind of sand or powder that had been blessed. He mixed it with what I guessed to be holy water, put some on me, and spoke a blessing.

He then said some very kind words about how these energies can catch up with good people. He spoke of Satan, of course, since he was Catholic, and gave me some prayers to say, which he advised me to say over and over again. Even though I had drifted away from the Catholic faith many years before, I welcomed his blessing and thanked him for his time. He told me that he hoped I would drop in and see him when I returned from Belfast, for he wanted to know how my situation turned out because he was always interested in this type of thing. I told him I would.

I had been raised in an Irish Catholic home, had gone to parochial schools, and had been taught by Irish Catholic Christian brothers. When I was a kid I had always loved the stories of Jesus. However, it just wasn't for me anymore and it hadn't been since I was old enough to make my own decisions. That afternoon, though, I was grateful the rectory had been in my field of vision when I needed it. I walked out onto the rainy Woodside street, feeling the wind-like energies blowing through my insides at almost tornado like pace and hearing the noise of the loud, demanding voices in my head, and I understood at that moment that whatever was inside of me was *furious*.

I really didn't know how to go on, but I knew I just couldn't give up. I was exhausted and afraid for my life, totally distraught as I walked down the street to my apartment. When I got inside, I called Trevor again, and thank God he picked up because I was just about desperate as a man can be. We got to chatting, and he didn't need to ask me how I was doing; he could tell from my voice what was taking place. I told him that I was in the worst shape I had ever been in, and I felt as if I couldn't make it even one more day. He said he could tell that the energy within me was very angry because I was coming to see him; it knew he was going to extract it. He told me to hang in there.

Later that night I picked up my brother Mark who was going to spend the night with me. He had to get up early for work the next morning, and I had agreed to drive him to his job. When morning came, however, he wouldn't let me. My eyes had begun to burn in my head, and it felt as if my muscles were wasting away. I felt really horrible, and from his reaction I knew I looked awful as well. He told me to go lie down again, then to get ready for my flight.

I was flying out of Newark, and for some reason I arrived at the airport a good six hours before takeoff; I think I was worried about what a disaster it would be to miss the flight. However, knowing that I had a six-hour wait in front of me once I'd checked in was a terrible feeling. I wasn't well—physically, emotionally, or mentally. I called Barefoot Bill and explained that I wasn't looking forward to the long wait or the seven-hour flight. I remember his asking me if I had my phone charger, and I told him I did. He told me to keep it handy. And then for the better part of the next six-plus hours, my friend stayed on the phone with me. I was truly falling apart, totally disorientated. My eyes continued to burn in my head and the voices were as loud as ever inside of me, tempting and teasing me with their wicked stories. I felt as if I was falling into a trance at times as I paced from one end of that airport terminal to the other over and over again, talking to my very kind friend all the while. I felt that death might have been very close.

I could tell he was really concerned for me as we discussed one thing after another: sports, Ireland, and everything in-between. He told me weeks later that he had been in great fear on the other side of the phone. He said that many times he felt as if he was going to be sick and almost had to hang up because something on my side of the phone kept hissing—angrily, frantically—like a serpent. Thank God he didn't share this at the time or hang up on me.

I remember worrying whether I would actually make it to my appointment with Trevor, the Horse Whisperer. As well, I was afraid that he wouldn't be able to help me after all. What were the chances of pulling all of this off? I was quite clear that my life depended on whatever would take place in Belfast with this man who I didn't even know—and that scared the absolute shit clean out of me. I felt tortured as I paced the terminal, and I repeatedly went into the men's room to splash water on my face. It was extremely difficult to hold it all together.

I looked at the departure screens and saw flights scheduled for Italy, France, Germany, South Africa, and so many other places. I was reminded of the family holidays we had taken when I was kid, to places like Spain and Portugal. Those were nothing but happy memories: kicking my ball around on the beach, wearing my Celtic jersey, not having a worry in the world. What I would have given to be a carefree kid once more . . . I wondered whether I would make the same choices if given another crack at life.

At one point, my flight was delayed, and when I saw this on the departure screen I became very aggravated. Enough already! I stood up, walked down to the duty-free shop, and bought a bottle of good Kentucky bourbon. *What the hell*, I thought. *Trevor is probably going to save my life; the least I can do is buy him what he asked for.* It felt strange to be buying booze in my condition, however, I tucked it into my backpack.

Finally, sometime later, I lined up to board my flight. As I did so, I had the sense that I was boarding a flight that would deliver me to the meeting that would shape my destiny forever. Unsurprisingly, it proved to be the most uncomfortable flight I have ever taken. Despite the melatonin I took in hopes that I would be able to sleep some part of the way, I couldn't get comfortable and twisted and turned for the duration, nodding off for perhaps only ten or twenty minutes at best.

I thought about my childhood in Belfast and the dreams I'd had while growing up. I thought about playing football, and the hurling matches I'd played in Falls Park and Casement Park and meeting up with my friends afterward to go out for the night; it was all coming back to me. I thought about what I would say to my dad when we saw each other at the airport. On and on, thoughts rolled through my mind, until it was nearly time to touch down, once more, on Irish soil.

Chapter 4
Early Days in Belfast

I walked out of my house on Glen Road in the Coolnasilla area of West Belfast, which my family and I had lived in for nearly three years. It was May 5, 1981, and my grandmother informed me that Bobby Sands had just died. After sixty-six days on a hunger strike, Bobby had passed away in the Maze Prison. I had followed these events every day on the news; I was intrigued by it all. Everyone else was too. I was less than two weeks away from being seven years old.

Over the next few months, nine more young Irishmen from around the north of Ireland would make the supreme sacrifice— they would follow Bobby—starving themselves to death in defiance of the British government, claiming they were political prisoners, not criminals. They really died for love of their country, having been left to rot and starve by Margret Thatcher and her British government. These men would become renowned throughout the world, becoming known as the "Ten Hunger Strikers."

The conflict with the British in Ireland had been going on for centuries—over eight hundred years. I loved reading the history books and learning about all the different characters that had been involved down through time. I didn't have to read the history books, however, to see what was happening in my own country in the twentieth century. I was born in 1974 at the height of the Troubles and lived in West Belfast right through them until they came to an end in 1997.

Many of my readers will be familiar with the history of the British in Ireland but many will not. The British had initially invaded Ireland in 1169 and have been a presence there since that time. 1609 was the official beginning of the Plantations of Ulster, which was a province of Ireland. Most of the colonists came from Scotland and England and were mainly Protestant. While the Plantations began in 1609, an estimated half a million acres of Ulster counties were confiscated from Gaelic chiefs. A lot of these Irish people had fled from Ireland for mainland Europe in 1607 in what is known as the Flight of Earls.

King James of England wanted the Plantations to be an enforced project that would settle mostly Scottish and English Protestants in Ulster, a land that was predominantly Gaelic-speaking Irish who were of the Catholic faith. In the 1640s the Ulster area was thrown into turmoil and civil wars raged in Ireland. The Irish rebelled against the planters and there were twelve years of bloody war, one of the many times the Irish rebelled against the British oppressors. This is the genesis of the problems between the British and the Irish and would lead to the thirty years of violence that were widely known as "the Troubles."

In 1649 Oliver Cromwell invaded Ireland with a campaign of terror during which thousands of Irish were slain as a result. Women and children were sent abroad to serve as slaves in foreign countries, many to places like Virginia and New England. Roughly a million more Irish emigrated during the Potato Famine, which lasted from 1845 to 1848. During this time, another one million people perished from starvation and/or disease. The British would see to it that their own neighboring country did not experience famine as the Irish did. On Easter Sunday in 1916 the Irish rose in Dublin and went to war against their British oppressors once more; the majority of the Irish leaders were killed by English execution firing squads when the outbreak was over.

In 1921 Ireland signed a treaty with the British, which gave England governance over six counties in the north of the country. The split over the treaty led to a very vicious civil war as anti-treaty forces moved into open hostilities with the newly formed Irish government. Michael Collins, who was one of the treaty negotiators, was later ambushed and killed.

The latest Troubles in the north of Ireland began at a civil rights march in County Derry on October 5, 1968. The mandate of the march was to put an end to the discrimination against Irish Catholics. This was the beginning of the Battle of the Bogside in County

Derry. In Belfast, the Catholic minority were unprotected and greatly outnumbered by crowds of loyalists coming from some of the Protestant areas of Belfast, burning the Catholics from their homes.

This escalation of conflicts between the Catholics and Protestants led to the British government deploying the British Army onto the streets of Belfast to accompany the British police force, the RUC, with the British propaganda machine making it appear that the army was protecting the Irish Catholic people from the loyalist crowds.

The IRA reorganized in 1969 to protect the nationalist Catholic people from the loyalist attacks on their community. The IRA decided that this was a great chance to bring the war right to the British Army and government, given that they were now right on their very own doorstep on the streets of the north of Ireland. On the other side of the community, the loyalist paramilitary group, the UVF, (Ulster Volunteers Force) had already formed in 1966, with another loyalist paramilitary group, the UDA, which means Ulster Defense Association, following them in 1972. These groups were made up of loyalists who prowled the streets of the north looking for Irish republicans to kill but generally just settling for innocent Catholics instead. Along with the RUC, (the previously mentioned British police force that had been formed in 1922), these were the key groups that participated in the Troubles.

Over the thirty-year course of the Troubles, over thirty-six hundred people were killed and thousands more were injured. A lot of innocent people were part of that number on both sides of the community. Thankfully, on April 10, 1998, the Belfast agreement was put in place. It was an agreement that took place on Good Friday and was also known as the Good Friday Agreement. It was a pact between the British and Irish governments and most of the political parties in Northern Ireland. It was an end to many centuries of bloodshed on the little island of Ireland.

The British Army was on the streets of Belfast every day, alongside the British police force (RUC). I could hear dogs barking and I would look out and see the Brits walking down the street, pointing their long guns and peering through the rifle lens into the distance. I was so used to seeing them that I could recognize from the different colors of their hats whether they were paratroopers or from a Scots regiment. I could even tell by their accents what part of Britain they were from. Often they would stick their heads into my dad's car to ask for his license when we'd be stopped at a checkpoint on the road coming home from school.

If I went out for a spin in the car with my mate Emmet and his father we were always quite sure to get stopped by them; they seemed to follow his father around and he had iron gates built onto the staircase in his house to stop them coming in and killing him when he slept. Back then I couldn't walk down the street without running into them but I just took their presence for granted. There were even times when I would walk out my front door and they would be crouched down behind the wall in our front garden.

*

Out on the streets of Belfast that evening in May of 1981 the tension in the air could be cut with a knife. Everyone was talking about the death of Bobby Sands, and the steel lids of trash bins throughout the neighborhood rattled in a thunderous racket of protest; his death should never have been allowed to happen. I could hear the racket from all directions but the loudest of it came from De La Salle School, which was at the back of my house. I went up to our attic and stuck my head out a window to see if I could get a view of anything brewing. I could sense the people's anger and frustration; an uneasy mist hovered in the Belfast air.

This was unique type of haze that appeared over Belfast back then. At any given time, I could almost "smell" trouble from the moment I walked out onto the street. I have never felt that unique Belfast dim smog anywhere else I have ever been and I consider it as much a part of Belfast as I do the old men with their Paddy hats walking down the Falls Road and into their local bar to have a Guinness, or even the two big iconic yellow Harland and Wolf cranes in the dock area of the city.

That May day I went to Bobby's funeral and watched the IRA fire a volley of shots over his coffin. I then walked very slowly with the massive cortège down Andersonstown Road toward Milltown Cemetery. I had never seen so many people in my entire life. Reportedly there were over 100,000 in attendance, joined by the world's press—all of this right on my back doorstep!

With my mother, I later attended funerals of other "Hunger Strikers" (those of the men from my community, anyway). Kireran Doherty was buried out of my parish at "St. Teresa's" Church. I would watch anxiously as the dead men's coffins were carried down the road on the shoulders of their comrades, who were dressed in full military uniforms, with masks and scarves covering their faces. I recall the intense atmosphere at these IRA funerals and fearing for my life when the British Army would attack the corteges and fire shots. I would have conversations with anyone that would indulge me about all these goings-on; I had so many questions as a kid. Why the military uniforms? Why the volley of shots over the coffins? Despite my questions, I wasn't confused about the situation—I remember grasping the dynamics and the politics of what was happening even given my young age. There was something in the military presence of the IRA that impressed me even as a lad; I had admiration for their cause. They represented the underdog and fought back against the might of the British Empire, trying to liberate old Ireland.

The scenes that were to follow over the next months and years would be flashed on TV screens all around the globe. Watching what was happening around me would leave an indelible mark in my mind. I grew up in the midst of street combat, sometimes intense heavy rioting, bombings, and shootings. Most kids that do stop viewing life through the lens of innocence and begin to see life through the lens of ego. I would be no exception and neither would most of the kids around me.

* * *

One of the great things about the people of Belfast is that no matter how badly they were mistreated they would always stick together and try to take things in stride. I remember lots of brave people who stood up and fought back no matter what. Irish people are very strong, hearty folks; real people who have real struggles. I feel lucky to have been protected and sheltered in many ways in my younger days, especially being the youngest of five siblings.

My grandmother lived with us my whole childhood given that my grandfather had passed away when he was relatively young. My mother and father were both from Servia Street at the bottom of Falls Road. They'd been baptized in the same chapel and had gone to the same school, which was common back in those days in that part of the world. They have been married for over fifty years. I also had a big family outside my immediate kin—so many aunts and uncles and cousins! The Clarkes are a large extended Catholic family in Belfast and family is important to the Irish. It was great to be a part of it all, especially when going to visit the McGreevys and the McEvoys who were my other cousins. That was always a treat and I got spoiled when I went there because I was the baby. As a young kid I was always listening to what the adults were talking about, which was generally to do with current affairs on the streets around us. My listening to the talk wasn't always a good thing as I was a deep thinker—and easily influenced I might add.

My childhood was essentially a good one—even though I had feelings of fear and loneliness that were amplified the older I got. Although I would be able to keep these feelings at bay for periods, as time went on they would show up more and more. I always had good friends and nice girlfriends but still I would feel lonely. It wasn't until I was many years further along on the spiritual path that I was to find out that this type of loneliness resonates from a spiritual sickness that can never be assuaged by people who love me. It can only ever be comforted or erased by a reunion with my higher self.

* * *

It has often been said that a person is a product of his own environment—I would say that I definitely fell into that category. I went to St. Finian's Primary School on Falls Road in West Belfast. It was run by Christian brothers and was right next door to the Sinn Fein offices. Sinn Fein, for those of you who don't know, is Irish Gaelic for "we ourselves." Founded in 1905, it is Ireland's oldest political movement, established to assert Irish national sovereignty and self-determination and to ensure the basic human rights of the people of Ireland. It enjoys an association with the IRA.

St. Finian's was an old, monastery type of school that had existed for years; it had opened in 1901. My brother had attended it before me and I suppose my ma wanted to keep the tradition going.

The Irish brothers didn't take any crap whatsoever; neither did any of the other teachers who taught there. If you stepped out of line, they were quick to punish you. The brothers carried thick leather straps that were designed for the sole purpose of disciplining the kids. The younger pupils got slapped with wooden rulers on their hands, which were sometimes taped together with scotch tape. I started in that school when I was four years old and I remember being screamed at and slapped from the very beginning.

At the school I would meet some of my lifelong friends— Geordie, Jim, and big Kieran. Around ten or eleven I started to notice the girls and became very interested in having a girlfriend, and as a result, I always did. I have always loved everything about a beautiful Belfast girl—and I still do. I had a lot of enjoyment in this department in my childhood and even more in adulthood.

In any event, at St. Finian's I also learned Gaelic football, hurling, handball, and soccer. Even though soccer was frowned upon by the Irish brothers—given that they viewed it as a foreign sport that the English had invented and played—they would turn a blind eye to it at times. Still, they didn't want us playing it a lot. Instead, the brothers would yell at us to play it the Irish way and when they saw us playing it on the ground, they yelled at us to bend over and get the ball from the ground into our hands. We would largely accommodate them, but when they turned their backs we would drop the ball to the ground again and revert to the British style of play.

The brothers were from County Kerry, located at the other end of Ireland and a haven for the greatest Gaelic footballers ever. I suppose they were trying to create something great within us on the Falls Road and it must be said that our school did produce some great teams over the years. St. Finian's always had successful football and hurling teams and I felt a sense of pride being a part of that. It's what I enjoyed most about school, and in the end I think my interest in sports carried me through those turbulent years and helped to bring my head out of the clouds for a while.

Our school was literally feet away from the peace line walls that separated the loyalist Shankill Road from the Catholic Falls Road—it divided the Catholics and the Protestants. The Peace line walls were a series of border barriers in Northern Ireland that separated Catholic and Protestant neighborhoods. They were built at urban interface areas in Belfast, Derry, and elsewhere. The stated purpose of the peace lines was to minimize inter-communal violence between Catholics (most of whom were nationalists who self-identified as Irish) and Protestants (most of whom were unionists who self-identified as British). The first walls were built at the beginning of the troubles around 1969 following some riots; they grew in number over the years. The peace lines walls stretched in length from over three miles to just a few hundred feet in other areas. Constructed of bricks and Iron, some reached as high as twenty-five feet. Parts of the wall had gates to allow for traffic in daylight hours but were closed before nightfall.

I can vividly recall taking the bus to school, down Falls Road as early as the late seventies and right into the eighties. That was one of the most restless times in the history of Northern Ireland—it was the height of the Troubles. I would sit looking out the bus windows, taking it all in, collecting the data mentally—watching the cars and lorries burnt out and positioned across the road from the previous night's trouble, sometimes flames still coming from the wreckage. That was my "normal"—watching the British soldiers flying up and down the side streets in their armored Saracens and jeeps shouting in their different British accents.

In times of heavy trouble there was always the chance that the bus I was riding in would get hijacked and burnt by the rioters who opposed the British. Inside my little mind I would wish for that—as it might mean getting the day off from school. I don't think I ever got that lucky, though. It sounds more dangerous than it actually was, because the rioters and hijackers never would have harmed me or anyone else for that matter. Their targets were the Brits or anyone else who got in their way. They were all fellows of my district, making a statement—showing the Brits, they were!

Somewhere in the midst of all this, not surprisingly, I picked up the belief that Protestants were bad and would be punished by God for their beliefs and actions. I later found out when playing football with a group of Protestant kids that they were told the same thing about us! When you think about it, we were all being bred to hate each other from a young age in the name of religion, given that we basically believed in the same Christian God although we didn't agree on the different dogma and the differing paths to Him.

I didn't know it at the time, but the ideas that I would learn about religion and God at a young age would shape my life and have serious ramifications that would cause me no end of confusion down the line. In attending a Catholic school I was taught that being a Catholic was the only way to God and heaven. According to the Catholic belief system, heaven is part of the afterlife, and you must be very good to get there or you won't get in.

St. Peter guards heaven's gates to ensure that sinners aren't admitted. This was all fear-driven, but the fearful concept of a punishing God really had an effect on me. For instance, when I would swear, people would say things like, "Jesus is watching you from that holy picture hanging on the wall. You will go to hell if you continue to do that." Why wouldn't I be afraid of burning in hellfire for eternity because I hadn't pleased God?!

As a result of this fear-based conditioning, I was riddled with anxiety, making me insecure from a young age. I kept this anxiety and my fears hidden. It was something secret that I protected, given that I sensed it wouldn't be a good idea to share it in a society that seemed to have tough guys all over the place, who always seemed to be using violent conduct as part of their daily lives. Given the prevalence of this type of behavior, I've often wondered why they don't teach some really valuable lessons in school, like, what do you do when you are afraid? How do you deal with someone who makes you angry? Maybe this wasn't taught to us as children because our teachers didn't know the answers themselves, so the entire topic was suppressed.

Trying to work things out all by myself, I wouldn't go to the grownups about anything, which is hardly a good practice for a child. The prevalent social norm was that children should be seen and not heard. This is diametrically opposed to how children today are raised in the United States, wherein they're taught to express themselves from such a young age. I watch how a six-year-old talks confidently in a room full of adults, without fear of being stopped. The times have certainly changed, and rightly so.

In any event, when I was four I started to develop a pattern in my life that led to my being dishonest. As a result, I began to develop a double life, one in which I had a fearful inner life and a demonstrative outer one, comprised of actions I wanted others to see and admire. I also realized that I harbored a lot of resentment, especially toward the brothers and teachers for the harshness with which they talked to us and treated us at times.

And yet, despite the beatings that transpired on a regular basis at school, no sexual abuse took place there. I've spoken to many people who endured that as children; sexual abuse has ruined many lives and often the abuse can never be recovered from. That said, as an adult, I did have to do some work around the physical abuse in the form of school beatings that I'd endured. I carried a lot of shame and guilt and a feeling of violation for being beaten and humiliated by angry grown men and women who were supposed to be representatives of the Christian faith. No child should have to experience violence or abuse of any sort. It happened often enough in our class that someone left crying every day. When you're a defenseless kid it's a big deal to be dragged in front of thirty other kids and yelled at and beaten hard. It's a form of brutality. Thank God Corporal punishment is banned in Ireland today.

I find it interesting to hear people say things like "I was beaten by the brothers and the nuns but it never did me any harm," as the same person is chain-smoking cigarettes and drinking a couple of bottles a wine every night. They probably have never been able to be in an intimate relationship and instead are living in a make-believe world that exists only between their own ears. They have buried their traumatic experiences away like I did. However, one can't escape that stuff forever, for it shows up in areas of your life and relationships with others in unhealthy ways, along with all the other unattended material that's been suppressed.

Later in the book I discuss my work with a very skilled shaman, Janice Zwail, who helped me to process the traumatic experiences I'd had when growing up. Many people today continue to blame their childhood for their problems and are unable to come to terms with their upbringing; they can't lay it to rest. I maintain that some people just don't know how to do this because they haven't found the tools to help them yet.

* * *

It's impossible for me to talk about my childhood or my life without telling you about the football team I supported, how I came to support them, and why they meant so much to me. The Celtic Football Club was the love of my life growing up. Everyone had a team and I was fanatical about Celtic. The club had been formed by an Irish Marist priest in the east end of Glasgow for the poor Irish that immigrated there in the mid to late 1800s in droves to escape the great Irish Famine and its aftermath. When they arrived in Glasgow it was predominantly Protestant; the Protestants had the better places to live, they had the best jobs, and basically had the run of the land—the Irish immigrants were treated like second- class citizens, which was no different from Belfast really.

These Irish immigrants were forced into slums where they were met with inhumane living conditions, unemployment, and starvation, which stared them in the face every day as they lined up in soup kitchens to be fed. In the poverty-stricken east end resided an Irish priest who was known by his religious name, "Brother Walfrid." The brother was from County Sligo in Ireland. He decided to form a football team to raise funds for the poor and deprived who lived in Glasgow's east end. In 1887, the Celtic Football Club was constituted and the rest is history. They played their first official match in 1888, beating the Glasgow Rangers 5–2; they would become the biggest rivalry in football. Celtic would evolve into one of the great iconic footballing institutions of the world and remain so to this day.

I was born to be a Celtic fan. They embodied everything Irish, and sure as hell gave me hope, and dreams to dream growing up. The Celtic tradition had been passed on by my father to me and my brother and sisters. It was in my blood and my daughter and nephews and nieces carry on that tradition today. It was way more than just a football team; it was a way of life. It was a way to communicate and spend time with people you cared about and it affected nearly everything about me. It determined what newspaper I bought, who I chose as my close friends, and it played a part in my religion and the social aspects of my life.

I don't know what my childhood would have looked like without it. In 1977 when I was three years old, I was led down the road on my brother Mark's shoulders. It was Halloween and I was dressed in my full Celtic kit. We were stopped by the local parish priest and I was asked what my name was. I replied that my name was Kenny Dalgleish; he was the star Celtic player at that time! As you can see, I was totally obsessed with the team from an early age—but most real Celtic fans understand that.

My dad brought me to my first Celtic game when I was four years old. I got carried away by it all—it hooked me from the very start. Religion and politics were never too far away from anything in this part of the world, and the sporting arena was a place to exploit one's political leanings at every opportunity. It was about the rivalry with our counterparts, the "Glasgow Rangers," who resided at the other end of Glasgow. They were the Protestant team, followed by the Bluenoses, who were steeped in anti-Catholic beliefs. They despised everything that Celtic stood for and were connected with, namely Catholicism and Irish republicanism. Like Celtic, they had a large following in the north of Ireland, from the loyalist side of the community, and they had a policy that Catholics couldn't play for their team. The rivalry was filled with bitterness and hate back then—it's still perhaps the largest rivalry in football to this day. The games would be battles, and on the terraces riots and clashes between fans took place. There were slashings and stabbings, pitch invasions, and referees were attacked. Many fans were also killed over the years.

When I was a young lad I reveled in the bigotry and hatred, which was more of a way of entertaining myself than anything. Besides, everyone else seemed like they were engaged for the same reason. However, it's a very dangerous form of entertainment because people get hurt and killed with that sort of stuff, while the instigators invariably go home unscathed. I wouldn't say I was a real bigot at heart and I definitely didn't have anything against ordinary Protestant people. To be honest, I actually saw their point about some of the things they found objectionable about the Catholic faith. I know that's blasphemy where I come from but I don't care; today, I call things the way I see them.

Brother Walfrid may have formed a football team to feed the poor in the late 1800s but his decision gave purpose to many other people's lives, none more so than mine. The Celtic team is in my heart and soul and will be forever. I still watch all their games on TV and when I visit home I still travel on the ferry to Scotland to go to their games, just like I did in the good old days.

* * *

My infatuation with booze had been with me since I was a young boy. I dabbled in it from as far back as I can remember. I always wanted to know what the big fuss was about; why the adults got to drink booze and kids had to drink juice. I remember asking the adults these sorts of questions when I was a kid, for the whole issue of alcohol had created some curiosity within my already super-active mind. I really wanted to know what it felt like to get drunk.

On a family holiday in Salou, Spain, when I was around eight or nine years old, we were visiting a vineyard, and down in the cellars the adults were sampling the local wine. I decided to join the wine tasting by knocking a few back myself. Well, that was the first time I ever lost my legs underneath me! I had scattered experiences like this growing up, as I continued to flirt with what getting drunk might feel like.

When I was a kid I loved the Christmas and social parties. At these, I always found it very interesting how people would loosen up and begin to have a good time and be a lot merrier after a few drinks. There is something in the Irish soul that seems to encourage alcoholism. If drinking was an Olympic sport no one would beat the Irish, for again there is something very peculiar about the Irishman's relationship with booze. That said, I realize that the problem runs much deeper than just booze.

Belfast was always a town of street drunks. They all stood around the road I lived on, and were ever present as one made one's way to the city center. We called them "winos' because they drank cheap bottles of wine such as Mundays and QC. I could tell when they got their dole checks because there would be half-empty green bottles strewn around them. They'd be singing, fighting with each other, or talking to someone who obviously was not there. When they had no money, they would say things like "Have you got a few coppers son?" Or "Any spare change, kid?" I'd always feel sorry for them, for they were out on the street drinking in all kinds of weather, sometimes alone, other times passing a bottle between them. Drunks seem to stick with other drunks no matter what rung of the social ladder they're on. I've seen this with bums on skid row to top bankers in New York City.

On my way into school I would have a good stare and often take in the sight of a female drunk standing on the street in dirty clothes with a black eye and her face smashed in. Invariably she would be standing beside another drunk who had probably caused the injuries—tangible consequences of a horrible, evil illness. Some of the other kids were dicks and would say mean things to them. I would always flip the drunks a coin if I had an extra one or give them one of the sandwiches that my mother had made me.

Sometimes on a Saturday morning my father and mother would take me into town. When we did this, we would always stop on Castle Street where the drunks were. My father would give them money and talk to a few of them. He explained to me that some of these fellows had been his friends and schoolmates and he used to go to the dances with them when he was younger. My da would never pass any of those men without stopping. As a child, I really found it hard to believe that anyone could end up like that. Thank God I never did, even though my own battle with the booze was lying in wait.

* * *

My real drinking started on the weekends when I was still in high school. It was a game changer of my whole life and definitely another turning point, maybe the biggest ever. It took the remainder of what little innocence I had left in me; from the first time I mixed my first snakebite of "strongbow cider" and "harp" larger, it was game on.

One night, I was standing in a field in West Belfast with my buddies before heading into a disco on Andersonstown Road. For the first time in my life I was to experience a transformation that I found freedom in, even though it would only last for the night. After that I would seek to regain that particular sense of freedom and I would chase it until it nearly killed me.

There is a beautiful phrase in the Gaelic language for whiskey. *Uisce Beatha* means "water of life" and I think this sums up the effect alcohol had on me better than anything. My drinking was to start slowly to begin with. Initially I only drank about once a week, which I had no problem controlling. But gradually I was to turn my will and my life over to it bit by bit, and the sorry thing is, I didn't even see it happening.

Alcohol is really sneaky. It's the great remover. At the beginning it picks your pocket ever so slowly. In my case, my education started to fall by the wayside. Next went the sports, then the boyish looks started to go before their time. About this same time, my whole demeanor began to change. Alcoholism takes your money and it can drive you into dishonesty, where you lie and steal from the people that love you. Then it opens the door to hospitals and trouble with the law. It will remove everything that's good in your life and won't end until it captures your mind absolutely, but that can take years. When I was a kid, I watched a man who lived down the street from my house lose his sanity completely. He digressed from being a happy family man who lost his beautiful family and ended up walking around the street in his bare feet, rolling around the road, talking only to the dogs around him; he was that far gone.

If anyone had approached me and tried to tell me that I was on the slippery slope to alcoholism, it would have fallen on deaf ears. When I was young I thought I had all the answers. I certainly didn't believe that the hardships of alcoholism or addiction would fall on my lap, and if they did I would see it coming and be clever enough to pull the plug. However, it generally doesn't work that way.

In any event, why would I ever want to stop? I had found the greatest tool ever to erase the fear and dissolve the sense of separation that I felt from this world. I have often thought that alcoholism is in my DNA, but . . . who really cares at the end of the day if it's inherited or not? The bottom line is, it's a killer. It might take time and a lot of misery and suffering but it will eventually nail you if you have the bug. For the next dozen years I would struggle with and try to control my drinking habit as it would escalate out of control. I tried to masquerade it as everything I possibly could to make it and my life continue to work and to keep the party alive.

* * *

I had just about graduated from high school, putting the least amount of effort into it that I possibly could. I had no desire to progress academically at all. If it didn't involve sports, girls, or making quick money I wasn't interested so I hardly even showed up for class at the end and had no respect for authority at all. I was enjoying being young and fit, getting a lot of attention from the females, and the partying was a blast. I was definitely beginning to enjoy the booze more and more, as was everyone around me.

At sixteen I walked away from twelve years with the Christian brothers. I had a high- school level of education and a "fuck you all" type of attitude. I can now see the karma that this created in my life for many years. The only things I was passionate about were sports and playing football. I was invited to try out for a soccer school of excellence academy and go to college for one year—it had a very good reputation. It sounded good at the time but realistically a year in college was never going to take me down a path that would have any real value. I viewed it as a way to buy myself some time until maybe some decent job showed up. I went on the trial for the football academy at Castlereagh College in East Belfast. It was made up of both Catholic and Protestant students and that was a brand new environment for me. It was like a cross community project in a way, designed to bring Catholic and Protestant lads together in the name of football. I played a game and trained for a little while on the first day. I'll never forget going over to the predominately Protestant East Belfast knowing that the majority of other players would be Protestant. This was a big deal back in those days, for it wasn't that common. It was a strange feeling for me given that I had always played with all Catholic teams and against Protestants—"Prods" or "Huns" as I enjoyed calling them. Although on some level I was open to this new experience, part of me was very prejudiced against the other side and I didn't have a clue what to expect.

The first day went well and I thought I had played as well as anyone there; I went home feeling happy about my performance. The second day I travelled over to East Belfast to the junior stadium for the final day of the trials. Again we played another match and again I was enjoying it and playing at a good tempo. However, thirty minutes into the game I got sandwiched hard in-between two people tackling me and all of a sudden, my ankle snapped really badly. It was one of those moments that I will never forget. The physical pain felt like someone had put a red-hot poker in my ankle and kept twisting it. For the next two weeks I lay in a hospital bed in the Royal Victoria Hospital in Belfast, having had two surgeries on that ankle.

If I ponder my life I realize that there has always been something pulling me in two totally different directions. One direction seems so obvious that I try to follow it and advance—then suddenly out of left field some event happens to thwart the progress I've made. In this case, I had been picked to have a place in the academy but I couldn't participate after all, given the severity of my injury.

That was a very long summer with many visits to the hospital, appointments with physiotherapists, and sitting around a lot of the time doing nothing. I was in a lot of pain and felt incredibly sorry for myself and depressed at times. Belfast could be a funny place in the summer for a kid with time on his hands with nowhere to go and nothing to do. I would watch my friends play football on the street and try to participate on my crutches, kicking the ball with my good foot. But that would never end well as my bad foot would swell up like a football and the blood would seep through my heavily stapled ankle.

My parents tried to keep me occupied as best they could. My father had always taken us abroad on a family holiday every year but the rest of the family had grown up and moved on. My siblings were all significantly older than me, and I was still at an awkward age and hated tagging along behind my ma and da. My parents tried as much as possible to keep us away from the Troubles and provide for us as best they could. The highlight of that summer for me would be watching Ireland progress to the quarterfinal of the World Cup.

I reported back to Castlereagh College in late August for a week of preseason training, which would be at Colraine University where we would take residence for a whole week. I could hardly do much training in my condition. My ankle was very weak and I had just gotten off of the crutches that I'd been on for over three months. We all had our own private rooms but everyone was assembling in the foyer—so I joined in just to be nosey. It was an interesting energy, Catholics and Protestants alike—a strange mix that I had never participated in before.

Both sides of the community were actually living and training together for a whole week. This was so that we could work on our fitness and so that everyone could get acquainted before spending a whole year together in college. Football was a big sport back where I came from so this football school attracted boys from both religions and all around the north of Ireland. There were many different types of personalities on both sides, all trying to progress and maybe get the attention of a big club in the hopes of nailing down a professional contract. It was about putting oneself in the shop window to see if you could advance as a player, to the next stage, having one year to do so.

As mentioned above, I'd played against Protestants for my school team and for some of the local boys clubs in my area but living with Protestants for one week and spending a whole year with them five days a week and playing on the same team as them, definitely was a first. I was a bit skeptical about it for sure because I didn't know what to expect and wasn't certain that there wouldn't be violence between us.

It's ridiculous really when I look back on what was taking place here. We were two different cultures that lived right beside each other only streets away—both Christian—but we might as well have lived thousands of miles apart because of the hatred that separated and divided us. I remember my da telling me not to bring any of my Celtic gear with me to the school. I suppose he thought it might be provocative and get me into a fight. My stubbornness, however, told me to put it into my bag just in case. The first day of training the Protestant boys were wearing their Rangers gear, so I thought, *Fuck it. If they're wearing their colors then I'm wearing mine*. It turned out to be a good move, for it was all taken in good stride and probably caused me to make a few friends! Some of the Protestant lads wanted to swap me things for my Celtic kit but I wouldn't do it.

Fuck knows—it would probably have ended up on top of some bonfire in East Belfast!

Chapter 5
My Excessive Drinking

Things were really changing in my life. I wasn't that skinny, dangly eleven-year-old little kid playing football on the street anymore. I was growing up and filling out, entering into manhood. It was also the first time I had really been away from home on my own. I wasn't far away from Belfast but it might as well been a million miles. I was beginning to experience a turbulent emotional inner life that would plague me and haunt me for decades. At times things would calm down for a little while but then it would all come on again. This felt as though my body was filling with sick emotions that would hurt physically and fill me with depression and fear.

As strange as it may sound, I always had a feeling of not fitting in, despite the fact that I was popular with my peers and especially the females. On top of this I was captain of my football and hurling teams and I was from a good family. However, I couldn't figure out why I had this very strange sense of separateness from the rest of the world. I didn't feel it all the time, but the older I got the more it appeared to be with me. Although looking at my life from the outside you'd probably see an ordinary kid who blended in, looking at life from the inside out that's not what I felt. I felt as if I'd been delivered to the wrong place when I was born. I have noticed this trait with other Kundalini people, this feeling of strangeness to life.

I wouldn't understand this sense of separateness for many years and I've come to believe that others who feel the same way, not understanding it either and frequently suffering in silence, may be driven to take their own lives. A kid very similar to me that played on the same team as I did and came from a big Irish family ended his life one day out of the blue by hanging himself with no real explanations. In my case, I began to search for a way to stop this horrible inner feeling that would eventually become part of my cross to bear. It's easier to sweep it under the rug and find distractions when you're younger—perhaps I only needed a women's love, the right career, prestige, and respect. Or perhaps a ton of money or being brought up in an entirely different environment would be the cure. At my young age, I was already becoming exhausted trying to figure it out.

Today I can see quite clearly there is no void and never has been one, it's illusory—imaginary—created by ego—and it was fueled by an underlying anxiety that has been with me for a long time. Every alcoholic or addict I have ever spoken to has admitted that at some point they experience this uncomfortable energy within that feels like a void or sense of separateness, and they become afraid. When you don't have the right information and guidance it makes for a tough journey (most people don't have the right information and guidance).

Indeed, what lay ahead of me would prove to be a very tough journey indeed.

* * *

I finished the one year at college to mixed reviews. I had a lot of good times and I made some friends—both Catholic and Protestant. That was a first for me—although I didn't keep in touch with any of them. I can't remember there ever being any trouble over religion or politics that year, even though the Troubles were still very much going on.

This time in my life was very enjoyable even though it was the beginning of my slide into madness. I was always good at making money and got a job in construction with my friends who were all a bit older than me. Now that I was almost officially a man I started to drink in front of my parents and in the bars quite confidently. I had been drinking in public since I was fifteen, generally using a fake ID. These were great times, but the thought would cross my mind every so often that the drink was having a powerful effect on me and that I should keep an eye on it.

Things got a little crazier when I branched out a little and started drinking in the city center instead of hanging around West Belfast. I always enjoyed the town but sometimes I had to walk home because I couldn't get a taxi. But taking a taxi had its own risks: It was dangerous getting into one if you didn't recognize the depot that the cab was from. If that was the case, it was a better idea not to get into it. It was a gamble—plenty of Catholics got into the wrong car and never made it home alive. So you just never knew. There also was a terrible period of the Troubles when Catholic taxi drivers were taken away by loyalists posing as customers and executed in cold blood.

I got into a fair bit of mischief when I drank in the town. Often I would get into fights with loyalists inside and outside the clubs. I got lifted by the cops on a number of occasions. Sometimes they put me in the back of a car and drove me around for a while and then let me go. Other times I would be thrown into a cell to sober up. Most of the time they would let me and my mates go, given that they probably didn't feel like dealing with a bunch of drunken mad men.

Today, my nephews and nieces have a totally different attitude toward life, religion, and politics. Their social lifestyle is also very different from mine back in the day. With no threat of trouble or fear, they go places that I used to go. They don't worry what taxi will bring them home or whether or not they will make it home in one piece. Things that were enforced on me back in the old days, they don't even give a second thought to. None of the concerns I had exist in their world today, and they're just a single generation behind me. They don't have to look at the British Army walking up and down the streets or hear bombs explode. I recall being continuously harassed by the British Army and RUC. The constable from the Andersonstown RUC barracks knew me by my first name and would come to my house to arrest me on occasions. I'd been involved in a fight with him and his men, which got me locked up and an appearance in court.

* * *

I became a blackout drinker. As such, I would black out and then regain consciousness in a variety of strange settings. Sometimes I would find myself in the midst of a party in some part of Belfast that I didn't even know. Nor would I know any of the people at the party—or how I had gotten there. I came out of a blackout one morning lying on a lounge chair on what seemed like a boat. Once I had gotten my bearings, I realized I was on the ferry going to Scotland to watch a Celtic game. I didn't have any recollection of getting onto the ferry. Nor had I had any intention of going to that game.

I'm not sure if blackouts happen to non-alcoholic people, like heavy drinkers, but they sure as hell became a big part of my drinking, as did the crazy behavior, the fighting, and the deadly hangovers that would make me feel like I was in hell. In addition to the drinking, I was also occasionally messing about with drugs like LSD, ecstasy, speed, and hash. It was always recreational use; I never played around with the harder drugs. They weren't available and I wouldn't have been interested in them anyway.

When I hit seventeen, I really didn't know where to turn next.

I had no master plan or any other type of blueprint to follow. Instead, I looked around to see what direction my peers were going in. This was an awkward age to be a youth in West Belfast. The options for teenagers were limited. Many joined paramilitary organizations and landed in jail or ended up dead. Indeed, my best friend got a very long prison sentence at this time. Ireland has always been a country of emigration, and many emigrated at this time. As mentioned earlier, my own brother Mark lived in the States having emigrated there years earlier, as had a lot of his generation. I ended up continuing on with the construction work I was doing, and tried to carve out a living for myself in this way.

The fact remained, however, that something totally different needed to happen in the north of Ireland to give young people an outlet, and one summer in the early 1990s when the Rave dance culture landed in the north of Ireland via England, it seemed destined to fill the bill. This phenomenon was character-ized by all-night dance parties that were fueled by the drug Ec-stasy, which gave one a euphoric high and plenty of energy. What a change it created in my life and the lives of thousands of other young people! The first Rave party I went to took place in a for-est in mid-Ulster; it was the first of its kind in the north of Ire-land. I was bitten by the bug right away; how could anyone resist it? There were beautiful girls all over the place, and no need to worry about getting into fights given that everyone was so happy, what with being smashed out of their faces on "E." I loved eve-rything about it.

It was also a break from drinking in clubs and bars in my own area where trouble and fights often ensued. Some of the places where the Rave parties were held felt a lot safer, but eventually when they became really common and more people were attend-ing them, it became much more dangerous. This was because we had to travel to places like Circus Circus in Banbridge or Kelly's in Portrush—places where it wasn't wise to let anyone know you were Catholic, although a good crew of us travelled together and then stuck together. The Rave scene was also becoming more dangerous because all the hoods and gangsters and even the loy-alist paramilitaries were getting involved in it.

I was enjoyed the Rave scene for many years. I was glad I was part of it even though it got me into all kinds of trouble with drugs—enough so to catch my parents' attention on a number of occasions. I couldn't sneak much past my dad. He always kept a close eye on me, given that I was the youngest of the family. However, they all needed eyes in the backs of their heads be-cause I was always a step ahead of them. When I would get out of control my father would have talks with me and even brought me to see some doctors for help. I have come to know that I'm not a drug addict and never have been. I just got hooked on that whole lifestyle when I was younger. I might have been different if my father had let it slide. But honestly, I could always leave the drugs alone when I needed a break from them, but I could never do that with the booze—ever!

I used to go a disco in the Greenan Lodge Hotel on the outskirts of West Belfast when I was younger. I hadn't reached the legal drinking age yet and as a result, I always brought a fake ID to that place. The bouncers were assholes and they would mess us around. Sometimes they would not let us in, given that we would frequently show up hammered drunk on cider and beer that we'd consumed in some field on our way to the disco.

One week, a large group of us congregated outside the disco. We decided to march into the nearby Blacks Road Protestant estate; it was a little loyalist stronghold, just to see if we could get a fight going. We caused a bit of mayhem and wrecked a car. It was no big deal really—but I do admit it was not one of my prouder moments as it was totally mindless thuggery fueled by drunkenness. We followed on through to Woodburn Barracks and within no time the cops spotted us and came out, accompanied by the Brits. They chased us and after a mini riot, we dispersed and went home. Back in those days when you made it home you were safe and sound. There were no CCTV cameras then. If they didn't catch you at the scene of the crime you were home free—thank God!

The next week at the same time we all walked out of the disco I just mentioned. My mind was a million miles away from the previous week's shenanigans; I had totally forgotten about them. But as we stood in groups chatting, a car came down Black Roads and sped right toward my little cluster of people. It then skidded and made a sharp turn as a hooded man jumped out of the back seat. It was dark but it looked like he was brandishing a Mac 10 or an Ozzie machine gun in his hand. I froze as I watched the whole scene unfold right in front of my eyes. People started to scream and the car came speeding back around again with its door still open, hitting the gunman and knocking him over. That was my cue to run like fuck. Fear gave me wings as I made off like the wind with everyone scampering everywhere. I could hear them coming at us again. Spotting an empty derelict house around the corner, I sprinted toward it, running around the back of it and straight for the long grass, which I lay down in the middle of.

As I lay there my heart raced uncontrollably as if it was going to pop out of my chest at any moment, and I could hear footsteps and voices from the street. It was one of those moments when you wished you were laying at home in your own bed, out of harm's way. I lay in that grass for close to an hour before it was safe to surface and emerge.

* * *

The drinking problem just wouldn't go away. As it began to take over my life bit by bit I would try to fight it every step of the way—for I just couldn't imagine my life without drinking. The very thought of that made the hairs on the back of my neck stand up. It was inconceivable to me that a person could find happiness in this world without drinking or popping something into the body to stop the restlessness or the madness in the mind. So I just continued on trying to figure it all out with a very sick damaged mind, even though I didn't know that at the time. My reliance on alcohol was progressing and the clock was ticking but I thought that someday I would get it all together and sort things out.

I would awaken in the mornings physically sick from days of boozing and drugs but toward the end it was very rarely drugs. To be honest, I thought they were dirty. Drinking was always my thing. Sometimes it would feel like I was actually poisoned from the drink and I felt like alcohol was pumping through my veins instead of blood.

As I lay there in my own madness—filled with guilt and remorse—I would try to look back through the events of the night before to remember why my head was throbbing and stuck to the pillow with hard blood. I never knew what I would awaken to. Occasionally it would be stab wounds and gashes that I couldn't remember getting; a trip to the hospital would be needed a few hours too late. At other times I would awaken beside some strange girl in some strange bedroom and I wouldn't remember her name. Sometimes I would curse myself and say that this had to stop, but for the most part I would be trying to figure out where my jeans were to count my money to see what bar my drinking would be continuing at that morning—just to get a cure for the throbbing headache, you understand.

The binges and the runs would become progressively worse, and the come downs would be torturous as I would lie in bed trying to sweat it all out of me, wondering where my life was going, selling pieces of my soul bit by bit. What happened to the promise and ambition I'd once had; where had it disappeared to? Ah, well . . . I would straighten it all out someday.

I came off the back of a bad run one night; it had lasted for days. I couldn't drink or take any more drugs. I made it home somehow and found my way to my bed where I could feel the poison shooting through my veins and sweating out of the pores of my body and head. With the room spinning around and around I fell into a drunken-like comatose state, nodding into no-man's-land. Moments or hours later I was awakened by a hissing sound and found myself tightly wrapped up in a huge boa constrictor that was starring straight into my eyes with its evil yellow snake eyes—spitting its fork-shaped tongue into my face.

I scraped my lungs as I screamed loudly, looking for help. I pounced from my bed of sweat to try to break free of the snake, only to awaken my mother and father in the next room. A moment later, my dad entered and turned on the light, trying to calm me down and stop me from climbing out the window that I had broken in a frantic effort to escape. After cold water and reorientation I got back into bed where now the hot sweat turned to a cold dampness on the bedcovers and the drenched mattress. My father left the room while I was still trying to figure out if the snake had been real or if I had been hallucinating. I patted my hands all around the bed, looking down at the floor for the serpent as I dozed back to sleep.

Facing my father and mother the next day after a night like I have just described was always a tricky ordeal. I'd have to explain my whereabouts for the past few days when I'd been missing.

Going missing in Belfast had everyone worried, given the nature of the Troubles, and with me, no one ever knew quite what to expect.

For my part, I just wanted everyone off my back. I never knew how to communicate the madness with anyone and my parents didn't understand either; how could they? My father was cool, though, and had great street smarts. He was concerned and wanted to help me, but I was a guy that couldn't be helped by my family's love—my help would have to come from deep within myself and that wouldn't be for many years.

Nevertheless, my father would insist on bringing me to the doctor to talk to him, which I always found awkward. Here was someone prying into my personal life and asking uncomfortable questions. I was also sent to therapists and counselors, and put on pills when it was thought I might be suffering from depression. Depression always seemed like the only conclusion that doctors could ever come up with to describe what was going on with me. The pills would work for a while, then I would get sick from drinking when I was taking them.

I had gone through a couple of dysfunctional relationships by this stage. They had all gone by the wayside, and I'd been told by one girl that I was an alcoholic who needed help. She might have been right but I wasn't listening to anyone; I was convinced I would find my way.

I thought maybe a change of scenery would give me some better luck and new opportunities. I had tried London twice and twice it had ended in disaster, for my life there had just picked up where my life had left off in Belfast. I was drinking every day and doing quite a bit of drugs. To be honest, I was happy to get back home after those forays; I felt like I was drying out. As mentioned earlier, my older brother Mark had emigrated to New York years before. I'd never really gotten a chance to get to know him as he'd left Ireland before I became a teenager. He invited me to go visit him in the States and I took him up on it—with the idea that I would play football and work, and maybe learn something new and make some money to boot.

* * *

I found that I really liked New York. The bars were open late, the drinks were flowing, and the girls were everywhere. I was twenty-three and handsome with the gift of the gab—and having a ball, which seemed to be my most important priority when I was in my early twenties. Once again my excessive drinking took off into overdrive and as always I surrounded myself with people who drank exactly like I did. They weren't hard to find in the Irish community in New York and I tried to blend into that community in Queens, where there were a bunch of lads and girls from back home. In fact, every county in Ireland was represented. I played football for the "Irish Rovers," which made it much easier to find work. I made some great contacts and got an excellent job with one of my teammates who owned his own company. It was party time and I had no worries about anything else—I felt free and everything went well for a time.

That was until my old friend depression tracked me down and started to work me over. It came out of nowhere—with the feeling that I didn't fit in in New York, either. I put it down to homesickness and thought I would shake it off. But what began to happen instead was that the void and feeling of emptiness I was to become acquainted with felt like a thick frost setting in on a winter's morning. It became crippling and I came to a point that I couldn't eat or sleep, which made me very sick and I couldn't make any sense out of it all.

Here it was again! I seemed to be getting ahead, going in the right direction with everything falling nicely into place, and then like the ghost of Christmas past, this soul sickness crept up behind me to ruin everything. I couldn't function for too long without it returning to my life, making my windows of peace smaller and smaller. I couldn't figure out why I was in this position. It was baffling and embarrassing to be so high-maintenance to my family and friends. The fear and anxiety would be so strong at times that I would end up having panic attacks and feel like I was having convulsions. It was very obvious to people that I was having some type of emotional trouble. I felt trapped in a cycle that seemed to be worsening over time and it was very obvious to everyone. I was soon to realize that there was a lot more going on with me than just depression and homesickness—it was more like a deep soul sickness, which was to become ever darker.

On most days I found myself drunk. As soon as my eyes opened in the morning I would think about getting a drink, just to shut of the madness in my mind and cool down the anxiety and take away the crushing loneliness for a few hours at least. My mind was torturing me and tearing me to shreds every moment of every day—it was pure insanity and I was afraid what would happen from one day to the next. I felt a darkness and a loneliness like never before.

Again, I was baffled as to why I couldn't find my way in life. I just wanted to fit in somewhere and be okay. Why couldn't I do that? Many years of pain and suffering would pass before I would find my answer to that question.

I left New York drunk and took a flight back to Ireland, with two big bags of dirty laundry and not a dollar in my pocket. Back I went, to West Belfast yet again, to go through a trapdoor into another bottom. I felt like a failure in life and was certainly confused about my condition. The things I had been convinced would fix me hadn't worked and I drank to escape from my plight. That's a lonely confusing place as you check one box after another in failed attempts to find happiness.

All the fun had left my life and I wondered what had happened to the good old days. How could I bring them back again? Trying to keep a job . . . not showing up for work . . . lying to cover that up . . . borrowing money and not paying it back because I never had enough cash to go around as a result of the way I lived . . . on and on it went. Then there were the fights and bouts of rage when drinking, and lashing out at people who didn't deserve it. Sometimes I wouldn't remember who I had fought with the night before and my friends would have to fill me in the next day, often to my amazement. The trips to the hospital to get stitched and stapled became more frequent. At times I didn't even bother with them anymore, I just went back to drinking instead, covered in blood.

I think it would be impossible to sit down and count how many incidents and fights I got into. I do know that the situation became progressively worse and I had a few really bad fights that almost cost me my life. Normally, they were not about anything of any great significance.

I used to frequent an illegal drinking den in West Belfast. Owned by a paramilitary organization, it was an absolute shit hole and it eventually got bulldozed. All kinds of undesirable people drank there. Even the gypsies from the camp next door were permitted to drink in it and they were barred from every other drinking club in West Belfast and beyond. I was drinking there one Sunday night when I was approached by a kid that lived on the same street as I did. He was in a panic trying to explain to me that he had gotten jumped by a crew of men. No sooner were the words out of his mouth then we were attacked by the very same crowd, and I started throwing punches at people I didn't even know. Then it all stopped and they disappeared. Most of the people in the overcrowded place didn't even realize what had happened given that it was so dark in the den and the music was blasting.

We both agreed that we should get out of there as it was just the two of us, so we grabbed some drinks for the walk home. We proceeded to leave the place out the only door it had. (There weren't any windows for it was a cinder block building with an iron door.) As we left to walk across the car park we were attacked again by the same morons. A lot of punches were thrown and some wrestling took place, but they were absolute wankers and couldn't even fight. We lumped them up and gave them some abuse for their lame efforts.

When things calmed down we grabbed our drinks and headed toward home, which was only a fifteen-minute walk. As we strolled down the road dissecting the recent events and having a laugh, the kid that was with me yelled "Watch out!" At that I felt an extremely hard blow land across my head, which felt as if it was caused by a hammer or an iron bar. I stumbled to my knees as lights and stars burst all around my brain. I was really disorientated in major way and wasn't sure what was happening. I felt another thud crash into my skull, and then another. My instincts forced me to jump up to my feet pronto. I ran after my attacker but he panicked and took off when I went after him. I couldn't run very quickly and he disappeared out of sight. My head was throbbing and I was losing a lot blood. Taking my T-shirt off, I tied it around my head to stop the bleeding. As I walked further down the road I met a group of people I knew. One of the girls started screaming when she saw me; I must have been in terrible shape.

I climbed over the wall into my sister's back garden and went into her house through her back door; she always left it open for me. I shouted "Angela" all over her house, then listened as she got out of bed.

"Adrian, is that you?" I heard her ask. "Are you okay?"

When she turned on the light she got the fright of her life—so did I actually! When I looked in the mirror, I was a mess—totally fucked up. I got very angry and grabbed the biggest kitchen knife I could find and wanted to head back up looking for this cunt, but my brother-in-law took the knife from me and put me in his car. My sister gave me the top of a tracksuit to wear.

I passed out on arrival at the Royal Victoria Hospital and came to in the ER, with an Indian doctor shooting a rather large needle into one of the gaping holes in my head. While I screamed and yelled, another doctor tried to hold me down as I got my head shaved and my wounds stapled together. I was then transferred in the back of an ambulance to the "city hospital" intensive care unit in the middle of the night. The nurses and doctors wouldn't let me sleep and kept coming in my direction, talking to me and asking me my name over and over again. The injections were wearing off as was the booze, and I had a killer headache, which was throbbing. I could feel the swelling in my head and every so often the nurse would change the big bandage on my head as the blood seeped through. I'd had many black eyes over the years—gashes and different wounds—but this was pretty serious. It could have even been attempted murder, but it didn't faze me. I never even got the cops involved. You didn't do that in my part of the world back then—cops were scum. I had taken a really good beating from the cops and British Army one time, which had cost me three teeth a very sore head. I hated them.

The day I left the hospital I was cleaning my bedside table out and found a plastic bag, which was tied closed. I opened it and almost threw up from the stench. It smelled as if a dead body had been lying there for weeks. I looked inside the bag to see pools of blood that were still damp all over the track top that my sister had given me the night her husband had brought me to the hospital—disgusting.

Speaking of being sick, I know my parents were sick of me and my actions and I would like to tell you that I wised up and got my shit together but instead my life got worse. Although anyone reading this story can probably see what my problem was, I couldn't. It was obvious that I drank abnormally but I wasn't seeing that as the issue as so many others around me drank the same way. It was everything else. I was pointing the finger at life and blaming it and the city I'd grown up in. I had a way of guarding my stuff and not letting people in—until it exploded and everyone could see it. I continued to drink, fight, and live this way of life but I was running out of time. I could feel the walls closing in on me and I would become sad and depressed with a killer, crushing loneliness.

Despite this, I still had plenty of friends and a family that loved me.

With the illness of alcoholism comes a condition that's really difficult to explain in words to someone who doesn't have that condition they just don't understand an alcoholic. I would drink on binges for days and then in the intervals go to work and play football, attend the gym, and try to grab onto what looked like a normal life to me. I would make myself a promise that I wouldn't drink again only to break that flimsy promise within a day or two or even a few hours later. And there were also camouflaged cries for help, because I was generally never brave enough to come out and ask directly.

As I sat in a bar in West Belfast one Saturday afternoon with some friends I felt so low but as always I would try to cover it up. Afraid of what was coming next for me, feeling I was stuck and couldn't spring the trap—if this was living, I wasn't interested anymore. I couldn't get the suicidal ideation out of my mind. Thoughts of taking my own life were constant, but how would I do it? There was a dark cloud hovering over my life, which seemed like it had always been there but that wasn't true for I had had many happy times indeed.

I drank in that bar all afternoon and into the dark of the evening. Eventually, some other friends came in and asked me to join them at a club later that night, which I did. I can't remember much after that, but there was evidence that I definitely attended the club that evening.

I do recall walking home in the early hours that morning, feeling so low, an all-time low. It was the kind of low where it can't get any worse. There didn't seem to be a way to stop the pain anymore; it seemed to be part of me even through the heavy guise of alcohol. I was doing battle with the constant hellish chatter in my mind. Something inside me was coaxing me to burn it all to the ground. The very same voice that kept driving me my entire life was the very same voice that now wanted it all ended. It was reminding me how much of a loser I was and it eventually convinced me to call it quits. I sobbed to myself, for a battle for my soul seemed to be over as I made my way through that Andersonstown estate on my way back to my parents' house.

By the time I arrived home I had thought about my life enough and knew what to do. I went into my grandmother's bedroom where she was sleeping and found her medicine drawer, from which I grabbed the biggest bottle of pills I could find— the one with the most pills in it. I brought it into my bedroom and I started to wash them down my throat, then I lay back on the bed.

I didn't know it at the time but I had an illness that I was powerless over and would never be able to fix by myself. Doctors, psychologists, and priests couldn't fix me either. Alcoholism is an illness that affects about 10 percent of the world's population. Most people never find help and eventually it kills them or they end it themselves by killing themselves. Generally, however, they torture their loved ones and drag them through years of hell and misery first. The number of suicides in West Belfast even today is alarming. I'm not putting it all down to alcoholism. I'm not suggesting that's the sole cause. It saddens me when I hear of someone taking their own life, when talking to the right person might have stopped them from doing that.

I vaguely remember my grandmother shaking me really hard and yelling into my face as she dragged me from the bed onto the floor. My grandmother would have been in her eighties at this time and could obviously see from my color that I was in trouble. God bless her, for she ran down the stairs and all the way up the street to get my sister and her husband. I felt my brother-in-law drag me off the floor and lift me over his shoulder. He was shouting at me not to go and slapping me really hard to revive me and get a reaction out of me. I was out of it and can't remember going in the back of the ambulance to my home away from home, the Royal Victoria Hospital on good old Falls Road.

Everything was blank for the next while, maybe until the end of that night. Eventually, I started coming around and heard voices by the bed I was lying in. I couldn't see anything—I was too sick to open my eyes. I could, however, hear my mother and father who were bedside. My father was squeezing my hand and I could hear from the tone in his voice that he was really upset. Doctors gathered around my bed and talked loudly into my face. A female doctor kept shining a flashlight in my eyes, asking me if I knew what I had done and whether or not I was going to try it again. I felt terrible. The psychological pain was unbearable.

Everything in my body was very sick from all the drugs I'd taken, and it seemed like my inside organs were dissolving. My really close friends and family began to appear at my bedside with bewildered looks on their faces. I could tell they were confused by what I had done—but what they didn't know was the part inside me that I had never shared with anyone, for I hadn't ever known how to do that. This was a moment when my internal condition finally matched my exterior world.

A major turning point happened to me as I lay on this ward in that hospital. I came out of one of those unconscious states that I was drifting in and out of as I lay in that bed. Out of the side of my eye I could see my best friend sitting by my bedside. He had just been released from Long Kesh prison (later known as the Maze Prison) on the Good Friday Agreement scheme that had been set up for the early release of political prisoners in the north of Ireland. I checked twice to make sure I wasn't dreaming, for it had been a very long time indeed since I had last seen him.

He came right out and asked me what my suicide attempt was all about. I kept trying to evade the question but he wouldn't drop it and told me he could find me some help, that he wanted me to meet someone when I left the hospital. I agreed to whatever he said just to get him of my back.

I signed myself out of that hospital given that I was getting restless in there. Also, my family was concerned and making a big fuss over me, which I didn't like. I was holding them hostage as a result of my dysfunctional life and they didn't deserve that. I was really angry that I couldn't find my way, for I'd always considered myself to be someone intelligent and strong and able to solve my own dilemmas. Be that as it may, I didn't seem to have the tools to live in this world—I didn't have what it takes to survive life. And just because I lay in a hospital bed and made a big commotion of my life didn't mean anything had changed. I thought it was a good idea to go back on the drink the day I left the hospital—straight back into the bar where this whole ordeal had started. I remember taking off my hospital wrist bracelet with all of my info on it, crinkling it up, and tossing it into the ashtray, thinking to myself, *time to put that experience behind me, just like all the rest of them.* It's amazing what a few drinks can do to change how the world looks.

At least my desire to commit suicide had vanished.. I suppose it was a bonus that the ego seemed to be leaving me alone even though this was to be short-lived. A haze of darkness surrounded me and I couldn't seem to get free of it. I hit the booze again, and it gripped me by the throat in its evil way and wouldn't let me go. My situation was further exacerbated by the fact that all eyes were on me and that meant I couldn't maneuver the way I wanted to and used to be able to do.

The next few weeks were the darkest of my life. I was labeled manic-depressive amongst many other things—everything except what I actually was. The word *alcoholic* wasn't mentioned once. Again, the Irish are funny when it comes to their booze. Their relationship with it is closely guarded; don't mention it to us and we won't mention it to you. If you do mention it, a joke is generally made about it or it's taken as an insult when someone's heavy drinking is discussed.

* * *

One week after leaving the hospital I found myself very drunk and in the possession of more pills. This time my other brother-in-law took them from me. This went on and on and I couldn't escape my predicament, that is, until my friend called me and told me to get ready. He had set up an appointment for me to talk to his friend. I had forgotten all about it, and it was too late to wiggle out of because he was on his way to pick me up in a taxi. As I travelled over to North Belfast in the back of that taxi I felt so sick and depressed I wanted to die. The gentleman we were going to visit was a priest and a qualified psychologist who my friend had met when he was doing time in Long Kesh prison. I wanted to go back home but he wouldn't let me.

My friend and the priest greeted each other and spoke briefly, then my friend signaled that he would let us talk in private. The priest invited me into a room at the back of the church. He sat down and explained his credentials to me and told me that he worked with people in prison and in the community; it was obvious he was an intelligent man. He asked me what was going on, but I suspected he already had the background on my situation. He just wanted to break the ice and hear it from me.

I give him a short explanation of what I had just been through, which gave him the green light to just come out and hit me right over the head with a question that made it feel like the room had just caved in around me. "How much do you drink?" he wanted to know.

I thought about it and stuttered a bit as I prepared to lie to him. When I did speak, I shaved quite a bit off the actual amount I drank, thinking this would keep him at bay. It didn't, however. The number I gave him prompted another question from him: "How often do you drink that amount?" When I gave him a more truthful answer he hit me over the head with some real truth. He said, "You're an alcoholic, son. You need to go into recovery and find help."

I was amazed to hear this, even though I had heard it from my ex-girlfriend and from other people over the years. For some reason, however, when he said it, it pierced right into me. He was very honest and went on to tell me that he could offer me some counsel to help me through some of the problems I had but my real help would be in a recovery fellowship.

I felt quite fragile as I sat across the table from him. I didn't argue or try to defend anything in the way I had done with people in the past. I mentioned that I had a good friend who had been involved in a 12-step program and had even introduced me to it but I couldn't stick with it. He asked me to set up a meeting for all three of us so that I could make the next move in the right direction. In hindsight it was another of those pivotal moments for me on my journey, the significance of which I didn't realize until years later.

I made a commitment to start going to meetings and, like most things in my life, got off to a flyer. I went to meetings most nights and most days and had weekly visits with the priest. This had been the longest period I had ever been sober since I started drinking but damn was I restless. I felt like I was doing time; I couldn't sit in my own skin for too long at all. I was showing up for work every day and thought this was some sort of big deal that I should be praised for, given that I had the belief I should be credited for my newfound sobriety. I also wasn't willing to buy into what they were offering in the recovery meetings. It was too large of a commitment for me to make that program my way of life; I wasn't done with my beloved booze yet and I couldn't stop thinking about it when I was away from it.

Chapter 6
A Spiritual Cleansing in Ireland

I stood pacing back and forth in my parents' sitting room one Saturday afternoon. I felt like I was missing something and was so anxious that I felt that my body might explode at any moment. It was time to go back on the drink, given that my other strategies to combat my alcoholism—such as making money and going to the gym—hadn't been going so well.

My mind started to work me like a serpent slithering around the place, and the voice in my head told me I had been doing ever so well and deserved a few drinks. It told me in its subtle voice that the priest had made a big deal out of my situation and he really didn't know me at all. I mean, this priest drank a one or two glasses of wine per year, what did he know about alcoholism? As I rationalized everything that had occurred—the suicide attempt, the anger, the fighting, the depressions, the broken relationships, and the lost jobs—I rationalized that everything had happened because I'd had a tough run of bad luck from living in the environment that I did.

I deserved a drink!

* * *

Looking back, the power and the progression of the insidious alcoholic mind was galloping right at me like a wild horse. I began to drink like I had never stopped and soon I was to taking things to a level way beyond what I had known in the past.

That week, I was invited back over to the priest's office to review where things had gone wrong, where my downfall had been. I remember being hunched over the toilet in his bathroom dry heaving and sweating the booze out of my system. I never saw that priest again, which was a pity for he was a good man who definitely planted some great seeds in my mind.

As time went on, my blackouts seemed longer and more often—the fun was nonexistent. People in recovery had warned me that it was only a matter of time before I went back to the booze if I didn't open my emotional suitcases up and start to offload the junk that had accumulated during my life, and in this they were spot-on. I was to find a way to drink for a few more years. In the meantime, I obsessed about how I might find a way to spring the trap I was in. I was constantly thinking that should I go back to those people in recovery and promised myself I would go back the next week, or the next. Or that I would get sober "tomorrow."

I had battled all week to behave myself, and as usual told myself I wouldn't drink when I got paid on Friday. Instead, I would pay off my debts and start anew. This was what the tape sounded like every week, only to be broken by some flimsy will-power and some stupid reason to drink. I went to the gym to preoccupy myself; for some reason I was obsessed with fitness right to the end. My friend called me and asked if I was going out that night. I told him no, for I was "off the booze." But he knew me only too well and a few hours later I was at his house drinking vodka with him. This was the beginning of my last- ever drunk. Friday night was another blackout but I made it safely home to bed somehow.

Saturday morning came around quickly as I lay in bed hung over without much recollection of Friday night. I promised someone I would play a football match for his team and the next thing I knew, he was at my front door getting me out of bed. I jumped into the shower to bring myself to life. As usual, I played the game dehydrated and half-dead. I could hardly wait for the referee to blow the final whistle so I could go back to the bar and start drinking again.

I went to a bar back in West Belfast and stayed there until dark, when my friend came and picked me up. We went to a local club in the area, which was a popular Saturday night spot. I switched back into blackout mode for the last time ever, snapping out of it outside the club in the early hours of the morning.

Some girl was screaming; apparently it was her boyfriend who I was involved with in a fistfight. His nose was plastered all over his face and it was bleeding. I didn't know how the fight had even started but it sparked off one hell of a commotion outside the club. My friend grabbed me and put me into the back of a taxi and led me to an after-hours club on the other side of Belfast. We were greeted in the car park by another mass brawl, however, we just walked past the fight and entered the smoke-filled club to the sound of the house music blasting.

We got a couple of drinks and stood at the bar. It had become a very strange night—everywhere I turned there seemed to be trouble. I got hit on the head with a bottle in that after-hours bar. Someone randomly flung it and it cracked me right on the head as I stood minding my own business. I didn't even see what direction it came from or if it had been meant for me. Something changed inside me at that moment—I knew the game was up— it was over. I told myself what I had told myself many times—I wasn't ever going to drink again. This time, however, I could feel the conviction coming from the statement I made to myself: *I can't continue this life for one moment more.* I set that drink down and have never had another one to date.

I went back to my parents' house that night and went up into the little front room that I slept in. I got down on my knees and asked God, if he was listening, whether he could come and help me before things all came to a very bad end. I saw a broken man staring back at me in the mirror, but for a moment something came over me and I felt assured that everything would be okay. I felt an inner calmness and peace. I licked my wounds the next day and lay low, going over in my head, as usual, what had happened the night before. That's a horrible feeling, when pieces of the night are missing and you try to put it all together in your own head for hours. There were many times that I awoke and was afraid to watch the local news in case I found out what I done.

I made up my mind that I was going back to recovery meetings the next day and I was going to listen to what they told me to do. I think the most defining moment was when I decided to stop taking my own advice. I got a phone call from one of my friends that day asking me what happened on Saturday night. Apparently, people who had been at the club on that night were talking in his office and my name was mentioned. It didn't matter to me what had happened—I knew I was done with it all.

That cold damp February night, I walked out onto the main road and flagged down a taxi and made my way across town to a recovery meeting. I nervously and fearfully walked up to the door that I had gone through on previous visits. I remembered that the number on the door was 81 and it was on the Lisburn Road.

I entered through the hallway and two men stood there—one my age and the other a little older. In a warm manner they both asked me "Are you new here?—WELCOME!"

* * *

As the plane came in I looked out the window at the big patchwork quilt that was Ireland below; all the different shades of green fields on display were separated by hedging and stone walls. My dad and my nephew were waiting at the Belfast International Airport with hugs and half-smiles despite the fact they probably didn't know what to expect when they saw me. All they really knew was that I was flying across the Atlantic under urgent and very peculiar circumstances. Because I found it practically impossible to actually articulate my condition to most people, I had almost given up talking about it; I didn't have much energy to do so. My system was under so much torment and I couldn't focus on one thing for very long—my eyes were burning in my head and I had lost a lot of weight.

That night I sat with my family and told them, as best I could, what had been going on. I could tell they worried and had shed quite a few tears

Next I called Trevor, and told him that I had touched down in Belfast. He instructed me to meet him in the parking lot of a well-known hotel at 10:00 a.m. the next morning. My nephew Caombhin knew the location of the hotel and offered to drive me. I gratefully accepted.

The rest of the night I was a bundle of raw nerves. I sincerely felt that this man Trevor had the keys to my having a future or not—that's an interesting place to be. The more I pondered the situation the more I realized I was hoping for some kind of miracle, some kind of healing that you might read about in the Bible or some fairy tale. My sisters Siobhan and Angela were nervously abuzz reassuring me that this man would help me for sure—but how did *they* know? They were well meaning and trying to make something positive out of a situation that was difficult for everyone to deal with at that time. I began to fill with more fear and started to think I was on my last legs. It felt like this man was in control of my life and I really couldn't imagine returning from him without some sort of a healing solution having occurred.

I lay in bed that night wondering about Trevor. What did he look like? What exactly was about to take place? What had I set myself up for?

After retiring to the bedroom I realized that I would be able to sleep in as I had when I was a lad. Lying in bed, I thought about the many happy nights and mornings I would wake up to the sight of my Celtic posters on the wall—how my heroes would greet me in their green-and-white hooped football jerseys. I took a trip down bittersweet memory lane, pondering a life that had been misspent in so many ways. This was the room that my grandmother had found me in when I wanted it all to end. It was also the room where I'd finally hit my knees and asked God to help me with my drinking obsession, and He had answered the call. Here I was again a decade later, begging God to reveal Himself and come to my aid. Sober this time, but in grave danger and a broken man no less. Never could I have imagined lying in this room again, distressed the way I was—it would have been unthinkable.

The next morning I sat gazing out the front window of the house. My dad was up early trying to get me to eat something, but food was the last thing on my mind. God bless him though. That man stood behind me through everything I'd been through in my life and never turned his back ever—and I had put him and my mom through some serious shit. I actually felt sad for him because I could tell by his face he was hurting. He couldn't do anything for my plight and I could see that he really wanted to.

My nephew pulled up outside the house in his car; he was right on time. I grabbed the bottle of bourbon I'd brought for Trevor; it was wrapped in a fancy bag. We stopped at the service station on Kennedy Way in West Belfast for gas. Given that my nephew and I were always used to bantering with each other, the car was uneasily quiet. Neither of us seemed to know what to say in those moments. I missed the teasing and taunting we were used to engaging in as my nephew was always breaking balls. Yet I just didn't have the emotional energy to joke around; I was too preoccupied with myself and with what might be about to take place.

We both knew I was in a dark place and desperately in need of something that was out of the ordinary. If Trevor couldn't help me to transcend my condition that day, I think I might have been ready to give up—I wouldn't have known where else to turn. I simply knew I couldn't take much more of this torture at the tempo and force it had been coming at me with. I felt plagued, harassed, and tortured—I was well and truly done.

* * *

We were early for the appointment so we drove around the neighborhood for a while. I noticed that all the loyalist murals were still painted on the gable walls, and the crib paths (concrete slabs on the outside of the sidewalk) were still painted red, white, and blue—just like they had always been. This was an area that had been out-of-bounds for Catholics back in the days of the Troubles, and really still was. I recalled a time when I was younger, meeting a Protestant girl at a club in Belfast city center and coming back to a party in this area with her. If that information had fallen into the wrong hands, my life would have been in grave danger. That was just one of the many stupid things I did when growing up in that part of the world. I had pulled that move with a few different girls over the years and was lucky to dodge the bullet. When I was young I didn't give a fuck. There was a certain type of badge of honor you got from your mates when you pulled off those sorts of totally stupid things.

Even though it was nice weather in Belfast, the temperature had dropped. The clothes I was wearing were suitable for the hot New York weather but not for these cooler temps. I borrowed a jacket from my nephew; I wanted to cover up my tattoos, which clearly identified me as Catholic. As such, despite the fact the political climate had cooled down quite a bit since I'd lived here, tensions still existed and I had no wish to take any chances. I didn't want to attract unwanted attention that might get me in trouble in this part of town.

We parked the car in the hotel car park and walked around the corner to a coffee shop to kill time and have something to eat. We talked about football for a bit while we ate, despite my lack of appetite and belly full of nerves. Finally it was time to meet Trevor. We finished our food and headed back toward the car. Caombhin opened his newspaper and I grabbed the booze I had brought and walked over to where Trevor and I had arranged to meet. I came across a small garden en route and sat on the bench for a moment to collect my thoughts for a few moments. I said some prayers before I saw a car pulling up that I knew must be his.

Trevor stuck his hand out the window and said, "Adrian?" I walked over . . . Here goes!

He told me to get in, so I did. Trevor was a man in his mid-fifties who radiated peace despite the fact that his expression was often quite serious. He smiled often and rolled his own cigarettes and puffed on them while he spoke ever so softly. He had his own way of completely putting me at ease; a feeling I hadn't felt in a long time.

I handed him the booze. He was surprised that I'd brought it and wanted to make sure I hadn't gone back on the booze myself. I reassured him that I was still sober. Satisfied, he put the bottle in the back seat and pulled out a newspaper to ask me if I recognized the man on the front cover. Of course I did; he was an incredibly famous golfer. He proceeded to tell me the story of how this man, at one point, couldn't make it onto the world's list of top fifty golfers, but now he was among the best in the world and had just done well in a major tournament. Trevor mentioned that he had worked with this golfer but wasn't specific about what type of work he had done with him and I didn't ask as I got the point he was trying to make: he had helped this man make a major change in his life. I was surprised and skeptical but I nodded anyway. He asked how I was feeling—I told him I was just relieved to be there. He stressed that he understood.

He handed over a pamphlet and I gazed at it while he started to outline what was happening to me. He explained that we're all surrounded by spirits; some demonic, others angelic. The human eye cannot see or detect them, but ever since Trevor had been a small boy, abnormal events had been taking place in his life. He had a near-death experience as a result of a car crash and was dead for a period of time. After he came around in hospital he could see spirits everywhere he went and soon learned he had a special gift, which he specifically used for healing purposes. He had been doing this work since he was in his twenties and had personally taken part in hundreds of healings.

Next he asked me if I had brought the gold cross with me. I showed it to him and he nodded and told me to squeeze it in my hand while I closed my eyes. He then put his hand on my head and very gently started to pull it forward. As he did this, I could feel my head moving like a magnet with his hand. I sat there with my eyes still closed for a moment in silence. He told me to open my eyes and look at myself in the sun visor mirror. I couldn't believe what I saw—the burning in my eyes had vanished and my eye coloring had returned to its vibrant blue. I was certainly impressed at the immediate effect this man had had on me in a matter of mere minutes.

He asked how I was feeling but I was too stunned to speak, so I just stared at him in amazement. He next asked me if I had been hospitalized in the year 2000. I thought for a moment, then confirmed that I had; I remember this particular period because I'd had a few hospital visits. It had been right around the time of my suicide attempt. What he proceeded to tell me amazed me beyond comprehension.

He asked me who Patrick was—I didn't know a particular Patrick and told him as much. He informed me that Patrick was a forty-three-year-old man who had died from alcoholism but his soul was restless and didn't pass over to the other side; or to the light. While I was in a very vulnerable period in my life, and in hospital, Patrick's soul had entered into me through my psyche and things had taken a turn for the worse after that. According to Trevor, this entity had been with me, inside me, all these years. Even though I had eventually gotten sober, things hadn't seemed right for most of my sobriety. I put this down to other things such as growing pains and recovery related stuff, and a lot of it was, but at other times my emotional pain and anxiety seemed like cruel suffering; it was extreme.

He asked me if I felt like I had abnormally bad luck and what's interesting is that I actually *did* think something had held me back at different times in my life, no matter what I did to try and prevent this. Trevor's question leant some credence to everything he'd said up to that point. The only thing Trevor didn't understand was that this man Patrick had an Irish accent. Perhaps Patrick's soul was that of an Irishman who had been living in New York? Things made more sense when I explained to him that my hospitalization had actually taken place in Ireland. I was a regular attendee of the Royal Victoria Hospital in Belfast during my drinking days. Here I spent quite a bit of time in a dark and eerie ward in the very bleak period I went through after trying to take my own life.

I'd also visited the Royal again when I got clubbed on the

head and was then transferred to the city hospital. However, there had been countless other times that I'd ended up in hospital after a drinking binge. One time I got a really bad stab wound, then went home and lay in my blood all night and visited the hospital the next day. Then there was the time I was bitten when in a fight with some loyalist and I had to go to the Royal Hospital for a tetanus injection.

In any event, I'd had so many visits to the hospitals in Belfast that it would be impossible to pinpoint when specifically Patrick might have made his arrival.

Trevor then asked me if I'd been hospitalized the past December and once again I answered yes, more quickly this time given that this visit was fresher in my mind. Trevor went on to ask me who Geo was, and once again I told him I had no idea. Geo, he explained, was a nineteen-year-old drug addict who had died from a heroin overdose in a hospital in New York. Trevor knew that things inside me had become significantly more violent after this hospitalization and explained that Geo was pissed that he'd died so young—this anger was literally inside of me.

It all sounded fucking outrageous—like a science fiction novel. But Trevor had gotten the time frames right and the facts were pretty accurate and very realistic. Nothing he said seemed off. I had never met this man before and it blew my mind that he knew details of my life—details which he had no real way of knowing.

He then said that when he touched my head he was able to help the spirits of these men move over to the light. He promised that they would never again come back near me. They had finished their business with me. Skeptically, I asked him if anything else would be able to harm me? He promised that as long as I kept the gold cross or something gold in my possession no evil spirits or dark negative energies would be able to enter my soul; these spirits flee at the sight of anything gold. He warned me that they'd had a lot of control over me and matters would have continued to worsen by the day without an intervention of this sort. When I asked him what would have happened if I didn't come and see him, he insisted that I would have been the victim of an entire soul possession, and would have undoubtedly returned to the bottle or killed myself.

In a weird way, things were now making sense, for I *had* felt as if I'd been in the grip of something vile that was creating the voices I'd heard as well as the impulse to return to the drink. It also made sense of my obsession to find heroin, which I had never ever considered imbibing in before. Although everyone thought I was crazy and I was sometimes inclined to agree, underneath everything that was happening I knew for sure that I *wasn't*. I had watched other people in recovery be half as interested and committed as I'd been and it seemed like they were doing better than me while I was getting worse—and I knew there had to be some sort of explanation for that. I certainly hadn't found any answers in recovery circles, that's for sure—no one had that skill set or that type of insight into this stuff. I was glad I had continued my search or I wouldn't be telling this story today.

Trevor explained that he also possessed medicinal powers— he correctly informed me that I had some bone cartilage sitting on my spine from my accident. MRIs had shown this to me in the past so I wasn't surprised when he said this. Additionally, Trevor informed me that I had black lumps on my lungs from my drinking and drugging days and told me about a tonic I could take to clear them up. We got into a conversation about some of the people that Trevor had worked on, and a few of the stories he told me amazed me. I probably wouldn't have believed him if I hadn't just witnessed the power he had. What impressed me the most was the way my energy had changed. My eyesight seemed much clearer and the burning in my eyes had stopped as soon as he'd told me to open them.

He told me about a man who'd come to see him when he was on vacation in a different part of Ireland. This man's son had returned from California with a wicked alcohol and drug problem. He begged Trevor to help his son so Trevor instructed the man to bring the young man to him. He then proceeded to remove, from this young man, some of the worst demons he'd ever seen. That was years ago, and the young man had completely stopped drinking or drugging. The young man and his father were so impressed with what Trevor had done that they showed up a couple of days later with no less than a bus full of people wanting help.

Trevor explained to me that sometimes his work is not all that clear-cut. At times he had been forcefully attacked by demons that didn't want to leave. He'd received cuts and bruises and had had some extremely tough tussles with these entities. But, he said, for the most part they just want to leave and pass over to the light. Entities or restless souls can see Trevor's gifts and a lot of them come to him to be moved over to the other side by him.

Trevor told me another story about a woman who had come to see him because she literally felt sick all the time. After putting his hands on her head, he informed the woman that she was with child. This was impossible, she told him; she wasn't able to have any more kids and doctors had told her so. She left Trevor unconvinced, but phoned a week later to tell him that she'd just had a miscarriage. She was stunned but he was not surprised. These were just a couple of stories he related to me. However, I didn't need to hear them to be sold on his healing gifts; I could sense his authenticity and I myself surely felt different.

The "Horse Whisperer" promised me that I would be fine. The one thing he asked of me was that I find a place where I could work with still suffering alcoholics and drug addicts on a weekly basis. I was already doing this work given that I was a regular attendee of jails, detox centers, and psych wards. He explained to me that this was probably the primary reason I couldn't find happiness and settle down, but he assured me this would change. I tried to judge the situation honesty and kept coming up with a feeling that he was legit.

He asked if I had visited Ground Zero in New York City yet. When I confirmed that I had been there to see the memorial, he warned me to exercise caution. He'd been getting a lot of calls from people who'd been down there and were now experiencing some crazy shit. This worried me a bit because my brother was working there as an ironworker. (I sent Mark a text message about this, which I probably shouldn't have done because it freaked him out a bit.)

Trevor told me that people had travelled from Australia and England to see him and to be healed by him but I was the first that had travelled from America. I could see that he took pride in what he did. He was very real and had changed my whole energy—that's the best way I can describe the transformation.

He went on to tell me to be careful when I stepped out of his car for my feet would feel like sponges when they hit the ground. But he also promised I would have the best night's sleep of my life that night. I thanked him, got out of his car, and started walking away. He stuck his head out the window to ask me if my feet felt like sponges. He was absolutely right, they did! He gave me the thumbs-up signal, smiled, and drove away.

I walked back to my nephew in his car; he had been waiting for me there for the entire forty-five minutes I'd been gone. Once again I felt blessed to have the family that I did; I knew they would do anything they could to help me out of this mess. Immediately he looked me up and down and asked what had happened to me; according to him, I looked completely different. Carefully I told him that I had just had an exorcism performed on me in what was an amazing healing experience. He just nodded and concurred that that must be true, for I was definitely a changed man as far as he could see. It felt very reassuring to have someone else notice the shift.

He and I made the trip across town, back into the west of the city to my parents' house. I came walking down my parents' path and my father and mother were standing and waiting with the front door open. My dad knew by the way I was walking that something had changed. Shocked, he told me that he felt he was witnessing a different man than the one he'd picked up at the airport the previous day.

My mom has been a churchgoing Catholic her whole life and my dad is an old-fashioned Irishman, not prone to beliefs in phenomena like what I'd just gone through. He asked me all the questions he could think of before he decided to simply be grateful that his son's sanity was intact. (For the time being, anyway.) I did feel worlds better, and apparently the effect this man had had on me was there for all to see as my mother made her comments and had her questions also. My physical body felt like it had been recalibrated to its original state and I could feel the muscles in my arms and shoulders come back to life and expand.

My sisters, who lived in the neighborhood, contacted me to see what had happened and were very gratified with what I was telling them, although certainly no one was anywhere near as grateful as I was. That night, just like Trevor promised, I slept like I'd not done in years. My trip to the old country was looking like a lifesaving visit. I thought I was out of the woods and all was going to be roses in the garden once again.

That, however, would prove not to be the case.

I spent another week in Belfast with my family. It was nice to be around my parents and siblings and to feel the love that you don't find anywhere else. I was trying to process everything that had happened and let it all sink in before I returned to New York. I desperately wanted life to return to the way it used to be before I had become so ill. I never realized that was impossible, for I would never be the same again.

The guy that I'd once known as Adrian was dead, and everything in my life would continue to drastically change.

Chapter 7
Three Healers to the Rescue

The healing in Ireland had been successful in removing the entities that had become attached to me, and I enjoyed some inner peace for a while. But I found that when I returned home to New York, I did so with a whole new bundle of fears. I was still dealing with the injury to my lower back during all this and it really hurt and at times I felt quite ill and out of sorts.

Back home, I lay on my bed wondering what was going to happen next and would I make it through? What I had just experienced doesn't happen to many people and I clearly couldn't share notes about it with anyone I knew. Nor could I find any type of recovery program or next steps. I had given up trying to talk about my condition in recovery circles because it was just creating madness and misunderstanding and I was being given labels by others who didn't understand the first thing about the situation.

Thus I was left talking to myself and that's a dangerous position to be in. It became important for me to find support— sometimes you have to search to find that. I decided to try and get back to living an ordinary life once more and my first plan of action was to call up a girl that I had been seeing periodically. Surprisingly, she was excited to hear from me. The last time we'd had a date, I'd had to flee the scene; I guess I was under attack. We were hanging out at the beginning of all my madness back when I hadn't got a clue what was happening with me and things were becoming progressively worse by the day. She knew something was going on but I never got into specifics with her, for she would have thought I was nuts.

Picking up where we had left off, we went out on a date that night, but what a disaster it turned out to be! Not even an hour into it I had a wicked panic attack and began to get super anxious. I told her I wasn't feeling well and I had to take her home immediately. She wasn't pleased at all, nor could I blame her. It was a shame, for she was a very beautiful Colombian girl with a great smile and a big heart; I had met her at the gym. Quickly we'd become friends and she was a lot of fun to go out with until all this shit started happening to me. I just wasn't relationship material, with all the madness going on.

After the fleeting sense of peace I'd experienced following the exorcism, I felt bereft—violated and confused. I also felt as if my nervous system had been severely damaged—ripped to pieces actually. I was getting lost inside my thoughts for hours at a time, trying to grasp hold of something to make sense of it all, but having no luck whatsoever. I had come to learn that although I couldn't get my head around what had happened to me, I had to find a way to keep moving forward every day just to survive. I felt like I had to learn how to live life all over again in a variety of ways, or that life was brand new in a very peculiar way.

Finally, I called Trevor to tell him how I was feeling. He explained that he had rebooted my system just like you would a computer. And when he told me he had wiped my system, I wasn't sure if this was good news or not. My thoughts focused on all the good works I had done. Had those disappeared also? Much of it had been intense work that contributed to my spiritual recovery.

Trevor promised me that only the negative had been removed; the great and helpful things remained with me and always would. I was confused and expressed this to Trevor, to which he asked if I regretted seeing him. I had not—I was much better but not where I wanted to be, given that I was conflicted and still suffering. In my naiveté I think I actually believed that I would be back to my old self again and the scary incidents of my past would be swept under the rug. No such thing happened.

* * *

For the next few weeks my panic attacks and anxiety were

out of control—at times I feared for my sanity and the feeling of hopelessness was edging its way back into my life. Even though the voices had largely stopped, I couldn't get my bearings. Fear about the booze was raising its ugly head again, which scared me to no end. I had made a great effort in recovery and even travelled to the other side of the world yet this mindset was as strong as ever. I talked about it to people who were kind enough to listen but no one could figure it out. No one had any answers for me.

Every day I would experience major anxiety accompanied by crazy thoughts rolling through my head all day long. My life felt like a "living hell" that I could never escape from. However, I tried to show up every day and live my life as best I could. My situation had changed since my visit with the Whisperer but a new type of suffering had taken place—it had a different tone and tempo but it seemed never ending. It felt like I was undergoing some sort of strange new process but I couldn't be sure about anything anymore—it was all peculiar and very mysterious.

I still struggled to be alone even though I was already alone most of the time. At times, I was stuck in confusion as to whether I was under attack by entities again. I would ask myself if what I was feeling was residual energy from the entities or had that energy really left me like Trevor said it had? These were the conversations I had with myself. My mind would lead me down dark alleyways of thought, playing around with ideas of what those entities looked like and what types of lives they had.

My ego was having a field day with all this junk but some days what I experienced would be so hellish that I would walk the streets for hours at a time. When I was out of options or didn't know where to turn next I would take shelter in a church and light candles and pray.

In desperation I would call Trevor again, unloading everything unto him, but all he could tell me was that he took pity on anyone like me who had to endure such horror. He also told me to keep praying. I appreciated that he understood that this hadn't been easy for me but I was also unhappy that this was all he had to offer me. I had been praying morning, noon, and night.

Having faith all the way through this was unbelievably difficult but I had nothing else to really grab hold of. When I had been back home in Ireland, I could tell my mother really felt for me. She didn't know what to say or do, but she did go out and purchase every book she could find on Saint Michael the archangel, the patron saint of demon slaying. She had put these books and some other little relics into my suitcase before I left. I was appreciative of that and was willing to try anything. So every morning before I got dressed, I started my day with a prayer to this saint asking him to help me do battle—that's what my days felt like—a battle just to hold my shit together for one more day.

All the little tools I had picked up along my journey kept me moving from one place to the next—one foot in front of the other. I had taken Trevor's advice and was wearing the gold cross every day, for my mother had bought me a gold to chain to hang the cross on when I had visited Belfast. I was trying to trust that I was safe and protected; that everything would turn out okay. After all, the evidence was building that something might be guiding me. It was hard to rule anything out, for some pretty strange stuff had already occurred and I couldn't deny that, at times, I was receiving *some* spiritual help and guidance.

I couldn't deny the visit from my sister Kathy, for instance, which directed me to the Whisperer back in Belfast. As well, so many other things were occurring every day, which seemed like synchronized order from an intelligence from beyond anything I could see or understand. For instance, at 9:00 a.m. in the morning, I'd be on one of my long walks to try and escape my suffering, and I'd get an unexpected phone call from my mentor who would talk to me in a very deep way, which would change the course of everything. The phone calls and the emails I would receive from people in those moments when I needed them most made it seem as though something or someone was watching over everything. It was the same with all the healers that arrived in my life at exactly the moment I thought I couldn't make it another day, coupled with information I would receive about my condition that would fill me with hope.

One day short of a month to the actual day I had met Trevor in person, I dialed his number in a state of terror. The obsessive thoughts and fears were unreal; the anxiety was threatening to physically kill me or so it seemed. Logically I knew boozing wasn't ever going to be an option anymore and deep down I knew I would not return to that, but the anxiety was so intense I craved escape. Thoughts of suicide were racing through my mind nonstop, followed immediately by thoughts of my daughter. If this kind of abuse continued much longer, suicide might have to be an option.

It still amazes me how much punishment I took and still remained sane and semi- functional without taking a drink, a drug, or even reaching out to take shelter from Western medicine. If it hadn't been for certain people in recovery, I would have been screwed. They kept taking my calls and continued motivating me to keep going and to not quit. They opened their homes to me, and some of them even invited me to come live with them. Where else will you find that?

Now that I'm on the other side of the madness, it makes me laugh when I look back on some of the comments that different people made. They told me things like I was self- centered and couldn't stop thinking about myself. They told me that I needed to find a different way to meditate, which was all such inaccurate bullshit. There were even a couple of folks who told me I *should* drink! I can't imagine how that would have turned out but it's fair to say it probably would have killed me. These comments really frustrated the hell out of me, as did people's false claims about the exorcisms they had been through, although it was obvious to me they were talking about something different. I don't judge the people who made crazy assumptions. Most of them were really trying to help me. However, I did meet some dark people along the way who I had to get away from rather quickly.

It was my fault for leaving myself wide open, allowing others to dump their pearls of madness into my space. Being as desperate as I was made it difficult not to reach out and ask for help. It's instinctual to ask for assistance when you feel threatened; it was for me, anyway. I have learned through the testing times of my own experience that the people who had the real answers generally didn't need much about my real condition explained to them. My great friends in recovery held me together until I found the healers I needed.

* * *

Deep down underneath the obsession and torture I would often get the intuitive notion that I would indeed one day spring this trap I seemed caught in—then I could make use of this experience. I told myself whatever I needed to tell myself in order to continue on each day. Of course, no one ever knows what life is going to dish out but I had never forecasted a path like this for myself. Paranormal mayhem and psychic attack farfetched and silly to me; they didn't exist in my world. In recovery I had opened my mind a lot to different things, but this was all well off my grid of reference and everyone else's too.

I had greatly admired some of the elders in my recovery circles. Many of them had great wisdom, but they couldn't answer some of my questions. I had expected them to know what was up, or that I could find someone who could tell me what was going on. When that didn't happen I felt very afraid and isolated. I had put all my eggs in one basket. How would I know what the spiritual path should look like? It had been naive of me to underestimate it.

I called Trevor again as I didn't know where else to turn. I explained that I had no doubt he had removed the dark spirits from me but I was having an impossible time readjusting to life. I thought my problem had been solved. What was happening? Why was I having so much trouble? He replied by saying sometimes it takes months or even years for things to calm down. This was not what I wanted to hear. I wished I could cry but remember not being able to shed a tear. I became so over-whelmed and riddled with anxiety that I took to the streets of New York and walked aimlessly and alone to calm myself or find some idea to flip me out of the onslaught of madness I was undergoing.

Everything came to a head one day when I called my friend Bill. By this time, he knew my situation very well. (He'd been the friend who'd been kind enough to be on the phone with me that day I was waiting at the airport to fly back to Ireland.) On this particular day I really wasn't doing well at all, and I asked him to try to help me figure out some type of help. I actually told him I was ready to drive my car off the road. He reminded me that I was looking for an instant fix and to be patient. He wanted me to give him time to think about possible solutions. Here I was ready to jump out the window and this man was telling me to be patient! I went and picked up my daughter from school that day and brought her home; she was spending the night with me.

The next morning I smudged my whole apartment with sage in a desperate attempt to continue on with my habit of cleansing the flat of any negative energies that might exist. In doing this I suppose I was counteracting the newfound paranoia I had about negative energies. I had even thrown a bunch of my old belongings into the garbage after my visit with Trevor. Smudging with sage seemed to clean the energy in the air around me and had the additional benefit of grounding me.

For lack of any better ideas, I started to Google phrases such as *the aftermath of an exorcism*. I didn't have a clue about what I should really have been looking for, but even so I read through every piece of information I could find. It's amazing what's on the Internet. I read many stories, some of them about people who'd never made it through stuff similar to what I was experiencing.

As it turned out, I would be barking up the wrong tree, for a whole new spin on things was about to occur by way of help from my friend.

That morning I had to stand at the kitchen table while I was using my computer because I couldn't sit and focus for more than a few minutes, the rushes of energy coursing through me were just too strong it felt like a world wind at times. I was lucky to have a very well-behaved daughter. Fianna was very low maintenance as she ate her breakfast and quietly watched TV.

All of a sudden my phone rang. It was my friend, calling me to tell me that he had picked up a documentary just by chance— he thought it related to what I was going through. He had watched the entire thing and proceeded to tell me about it.

Wake Up, the Film is the true story of one ordinary man's experience of visualizing spirits. His name is Jonas Elrod and his story had some similarities to mine. Elrod awoke one morning with the realization that he could see spirits—some demonic, others angelic. He could see them all around him, along with a variety of other energies. The problem was that no one else could see them. After embarking on a journey in the religious and spiritual realms to find answers, he came across a man who would help to change not only his life immensely, but my own life as well. Before my friend and I had even finished our conversation on the phone I had found Jonas Elrod's contact information online.

I emailed Jonas Elrod within the space of a few minutes, eagerly explaining, in a very long note, everything I could about my situation. I was amazed when I received a response within the hour from someone who worked with Jonas. This person told me that Abdi Assadi was the person I should contact and that Elrod was currently out of town but would reply when he returned. Thus I sent the same email to Abdi Assadi—explaining everything.

He too responded promptly and outlined things that I should be aware of. He wrote, "It's a shock to the system to realize how such energies can affect us," and went on to reassure me that what I was experiencing could be a normal part of my process. "Understand that the entities came into you due to an opening in the psyche," he told me, which was exactly what Trevor had said. Abdi went on to explain that the healing process has to continue and does not end with the removal of the entities. That is just the first step, now. I had to dig deeper. He told me to sincerely practice surrender—"Sit with yourself and see what your next step is. You have had psychic surgery and as such there is a recuperation and rehabilitation period afterward, which is usually more intense than the procedure itself."

He told me about two people in New York City who could help me through that process. The first was Penney Leyshon, an intuitive soul healer and—as I would soon find out—a very powerful seer. The second was a shamanic practitioner of the Lakota tradition who performed various types of healing work. She would finish the job—her name, as mentioned earlier, was Janice Zwail.

One thing I have learned on my journey is that no one person holds the full answer to anything on the spiritual path or realm. Instead, the truth seems to be divided up amongst many healers and teachers. Also, plain everyday people may have some of the answers. Learning this had helped me refrain from putting any human being on a pedestal, no matter what their powers might be. I have been blessed to meet some healers with super powers, and what I find interesting is that the most powerful healers tend to travel quietly under the radar without much advertising or publicity—no Hollywood prestige wanted or needed by them whatsoever. They don't post talks or comments on social media every five minutes. Instead they have a demonstrated love and willingness to help those in desperate need find spiritual solace and relief. I've found that there is a silent army of suffering souls out there who are isolated from society. I feel blessed that the universe delivered these healers to me when I needed them the most.

Needless to say I reached out to Penney and Janice right away. Doing so gave me hope. I called Penney first, and got her voice mail. I left a distressed message with as much information as I could cram into it before I was cut off. I then called Janice, the shamanic practitioner. It was Thursday afternoon and I caught her leaving her office. I told her as much of my story as

I could. Janice was warm and caring, and listened attentively to what I said. I could tell she didn't doubt what I was telling her for a minute. She gave me a few pointers, some of which I already knew and had already begun to implement. And although I was interested in what she had to say, I was really only concerned with knowing whether or not she could help me. When I put this question to her, she was honest and told me that she didn't know, but that she would try.

In the meantime, Penney returned my call. She was an incredibly soft-spoken lady whose voice radiated serenity. Despite this, I learned right away from her first words that she was a tough, no-nonsense lady. She really read the no-bullshit policy and firmly stated that if I didn't want her help then I should go elsewhere. I explained to her about the Horse Whisperer in Ireland and my exorcism, to which she confidently informed me that she was the queen of exorcism. Her whole attitude exuded a sense of real power and I had no reason not to believe her. Penney earned my confidence right from the start, as Janice had done before her.

Penney told me to check out her website (www.Penneyleyshon.com), to take a closer look before deciding if I wanted her help. I just wanted the torture to stop, and thought *Fuck it, what do I have to lose?* I asked her if she thought she could really help me, which she took as an insult to her abilities. I felt like she might hang the phone up at any moment—although after working with her for a while, I understood why she behaved like this. She told me if we were going to work together she would start the process right away, which I did find strange, but decided to try to remain open-minded. For some reason I trusted her. Having no other options will do that for you—make you believe in the unbelievable. We set up an appointment for 10:00 a.m. the next morning.

After being in touch with Abdi and getting to talk with both Penney and Janice I had a strong feeling that these people were the real deal. This was the same vibe I had gotten from Trevor. These people had to make a living so their fees were generally always reasonable. I didn't think any of them were getting rich from their work and they all took care of me at times by lowering their fee when I was struggling financially.

There is a huge market of people claiming many things these days—whether it's in the recovery world or in the spiritual world—and most people are trying to sell something. I've learned along the way that there are many dangerous people out there posing as people with special powers and who make big promises as healers. When people are in a vulnerable condition and have no place else to turn they may run into these charlatans and scammers, who have been known to exploit the situation by taking advantage of these folks in a variety of ways. It may be financially; it may be sexually; and/or it may be to enhance their own prestige. My experience is—trust your gut, for that never lies. If something feels off about a certain healer, teacher, or guru on a gut level, then trust that. I have met many of these individuals who frequently come across as smart charismatic individuals; they tend to have all the healing and spiritual lingo down to a fine art. They sound like they know their shit, and some even do. But there can also be a darkness and craziness that accompanies that person.

I have learned that I should never give my personal power over to another individual, no matter what they claim. An authentic guru will always point you to your own source of power and take himself or herself out of the equation. And this is what you should seek to do: Exclude the middle man and tap into your own power, for you have it right inside of you. Thankfully, I weeded out the crazies and phonies pretty quickly; there were quite a few.

* * *

The night before I was to meet Penney was another sleepless night full of fear and anticipation. By this time I was used to watching each hour of the clock pass by as I lay there thinking into the morning. Some nights were incredibly hellish—I would walk every inch of my apartment in a demented state. One night, I even found myself hunched in the fetal position underneath my kitchen table, trying anything and everything to avoid the internal chaotic hell. I must have been making serious noise because the neighbors downstairs complained to my landlord, who then mentioned it to me. By 7:00 a.m. I would be up on my feet, cranky, but ready for another day of madness. I would think to myself every day, *Is it going to be today that I'll find freedom?* I was like a man clinging to the hope that that day would be the day he'd be released from prison, only to find out that wasn't the case at all.

I was looking for a quick fix but healing doesn't work that way. There would be no quick fixes to a situation like this and I would have saved myself a lot of time and stress if I could have surrendered to that idea. The addictive nature of the wanting mind desires everything now, and it becomes really upset when things don't materialize to its liking. I could see that this is where my suffering was coming from. I was thinking a lot of crazy thoughts and believing them. That's how it had been my entire life, but now this process had shifted into overdrive. In reality, if you don't believe the thoughts, they remain mere thoughts. However, I hadn't arrived at that place of understanding yet.

I arrived for my appointment with Penney ever so early, my stomach in knots and my mind racing. I tried to imagine her place, what she looked like, what was going to take place at our meeting, but all that did was make me more anxious. I paced around the block many times to eat the clock up. Eventually our appointed time drew near and I walked toward her apartment between Columbus and Amsterdam Avenue in Manhattan. I sat on the black iron steps outside for exactly seven minutes, waiting for the clock to hit ten.

Penney buzzed me in as soon as I rang the bell and I climbed the four flights of stairs to her apartment. A small lady dressed in black greeted me at the door; she had a big smile and bright eyes. She asked how I was doing and I laid it all out to her as she nodded, seeming to understand where I was coming from. I was

111

instructed to take off my watch, belt, and shoes and to put my phone and wallet on a shelf. I followed her request as I gazed around her meticulously clean, bright apartment. It had a very homely feel to it and was decorated with numerous paintings that Penney had painted herself. She then directed me to a back room and pointed at a table and told me to lie down on it.

Penney had been born in Staten Island, the oldest of five children. Professionally, before becoming a healer, she had worked as a human resources counselor and in the finance world on Wall Street. As well, she'd worked in a women's healthcare crisis center, which was to help prepare her to become a spiritual healer. By the time I was lucky enough to meet her, she had been in private healing practice for twenty-five years, and had helped to heal thousands of people from all over the world. Incredibly gifted but never run-of-the-mill, Penney was open to the workings of the universe in a way that few healers are. Implicit in this is the understanding that the body, mind, and spirit are always striving to be in a state of perfect health, whether we realize it or not.

Penney had borne witness to some pretty amazing spiritual experiences in her journey to become a healer. She had survived a struggle with anorexia, wherein at her lowest point she weighed a mere seventy pounds and she'd suffered a breakdown as a result. Walking in the woods in northern New Jersey in trying to seek solace from nature, a great light had emerged from the ground and entered her through her eyes, anointing her with the incredible healing gift that has served her ever since. She would go on to study Shiatsu massage for six years, which included studying at the Ohashi Institute in New York to learn the Ohashi method of massage—a form of healing touch energy work. Ultimately, she earned a massage license from the Swedish Institute, a board-certified massage school in New York.

When Penney was forty-two she underwent another extraordinary spiritual experience, as relayed in her own words: "I saw the Earth from the beginning of itself and past there. I saw the universe and past there. All of the past came flooding in and through. I witnessed it through me . . . second by second of terror and pain, mine and that of humanity. I became so alert that the vibration of sound altered me, and presented different realities that sent me into and through horrific episodes. It was a massive panic, and yet holy. It captured me. This period was devastating. Yet somehow I kept on functioning around it, in life. I got up, I ate, walked, bathed, but I didn't understand why or what was going on. I just knew that it was happening for some deep reason . . . some type of purpose. I knew that I must stay with it. It was certainly staying with me. Time for me has been altered and the work advanced." (This is from Penney's book, *A Gift of Healing in a Handbook,* which is available through Penney's website.)

Penney has an extraordinary energy and her eyes are unbelievable. I could tell that she had many worlds behind those eyes but I couldn't in my wildest dreams imagine what was there. As I lay on the table, she began to stare at different parts of my body with an intense gaze, glancing at my chest and gut, commenting that she could tell that the Horse Whisperer had been there. According to her, he had done his work very well but it had to be finished. She was able to ascertain that I had been full of rage and started to tell me things about my past that she couldn't have possibly known. To be honest I wasn't really surprised at all, but I did find it all very intriguing. I was becoming used to the fact that I was having a very unique experience with a group of very unique people.

She asked whether or not I had played soccer, which I had. That's why my body was cut up the way it was, she commented. Today I know that she was looking a lot deeper than that: her staring was seeing right into what was in the very depths of my soul. Apparently she was looking at my whole life, which was revealed within my body. It was mind-blowing to watch her work. At times she would become really nauseous as she struggled with some of the energies that were inside of me, or fuming off of me, perhaps I should say. She picked up on everything and asked me not to wear cologne in the future as it was making her feel ill.

There was a female energy that was gripping me tight and

didn't like the work Penney was doing. But Penney struggled with it and then moved around my body. She tapped my chest and told me to grab the energy and throw it out the window. I just followed her directions and tried to work with her.

I asked her the most important question that seemed to be running my life at that time. Why wouldn't the fear around the booze leave me alone, even after the commitment I had made to the 12-step program? She told me that the 12 steps were for my ego and what was currently ailing me was coming from the depths of my soul. She looked at me right in the eye and said, "Baby, your whole life has hit you all at once." It seemed true even though I didn't fully understand all of what she meant. She explained to me that the turmoil I found myself in 24/7 wasn't just from this lifetime, it was karma that had accumulated from many lifetimes, and it now needed to be cleared.

I had often wondered about reincarnation. I never had any proof actual concrete proof myself of past lives. However, even though I've had strange moments of thinking I'd visited a place before or met a person someplace else, I couldn't place that memory in this lifetime. I grew up in a religious system that didn't believe in reincarnation and I never really had any proof of it. It would, however, be a common topic of conversation with the healers I would soon be working with, and at times—when the intense energy was working through my system—I intuitively felt the presence of past lives.

On a subsequent visit with Penney, she told me I'd had a previous life in which I'd been stabbed and drowned. Later, when I worked with Janice, she had a vision with me in it. I was an American Indian hunter riding back from a hunt on horseback, dragging a dead carcass. In Janice's shamanic vision she told me that I was receiving a great healing from an Indian medicine man and that the Tibetans were showing up in my healing as well.

* * *

I have thought many times about what professional descriptor I could give Penney, but probably the ones that are most apt are psychic and soul healer. As I've done more work with her, I realize there are other healing modalities that she practices, most of them way beyond my human intellectual understanding. From my perspective she's a psychic and a "soul healer." Her work is no joke—she has an absolutely amazing way of steeping right into your being to apply the healing tools and powers she's been so uniquely gifted with. I have to say that the closest thing I have ever seen to miracles in my whole life were my experiences with Trevor back in Ireland and with Penney in New York.

I could feel an amazing presence and love from this lady, and at times I wouldn't want to leave her apartment because I felt so safe in her company. She didn't miss a beat, and ended our first session by telling me she would work on my back injury. We returned to the front room, and I had so many questions I wanted to ask her but I didn't as I was in a fairly altered state after what had just taken place. She told me to drink plenty of water because my system would be cleansing itself. Then she said something that really caught my attention. She looked straight into my eye and told me that she believed I was up for what would be happening next.

This really alarmed me to no end; what did she mean by it? I asked her if my obsessive thoughts would stop. She said no, but that they would get much softer. I was given further directions to follow regarding exercise and diet. I then thanked her and walked out of her New York City apartment into the sunny Friday morning.

A lot had happened in that first session with Penney. She explained many things to me, although she didn't tell me all that much about what specifically was going on. She did tell me, though, that she was working to get the rage up and out of the depths of my soul. I had been an angry boy for a lot of my life.

I left her place with a much needed shift in my energy and some sorely needed hope. The obsessive thoughts still had a very active life of their own and would roll on through whenever they wanted—but Penney was right, they *were* much softer. I had been learning to stop fighting them—when you do that it gives them less power—but sometimes that had no effect as they were frequently still very forceful.

My terror was still there, too. Actually, even with the introduction of my new team of healers, I was far from all right and still had a long way to go before I'd be out of the woods. At times I would call my friends just to stay sane when what I call "the beast" seemed to be awake and at its most forceful; talking with friends would help to preserve my sanity.

One of the biggest storms of modern times was forecasted for that night and New York was destined to be hard hit. I got plenty of supplies in and settled into my apartment as the storm they had named "Irene" was gathering force and taking control on the streets outside. I could feel Penney's healing work begin to manifest within me as I sat in my chair listening to the rain beating off my windows. It was a brutal storm for the city, but it would be short-lived. As it raged outside, I was working to come to terms with my own internal storm—and the many unanswered questions I still had about it.

* * *

I woke up the next morning sensing the calmness after the storm, realizing that I had slept pretty well for the first time in a long time. Something had shifted and I couldn't help but notice the big change I felt within myself. I hadn't experienced such peace and calmness in many months—there was still a lot of psychological and physical pain to follow but at last I felt I was getting somewhere.

Penney has a rule that no one can call her to discuss the healing work that has been done during the therapy sessions but the next day Penney called me by mistake. She asked me how I was doing, and called me "sweetie pie," which I thought was strange but amusing all the same. I reported I was much better and could feel shifts taking place. She replied by telling me that my soul had been fighting with her but major stuff had fallen away and had left my system. It *sounded* crazy but it all felt true.

Janice Zwail was the second healer I would work with. She and I had phone and text conversations before we met in person. This woman had a larger-than-life energy and I felt very safe around her, which is one of the ways to tell that you're in good hands. Her instincts were sharper than a razor blade and she picked up on every word I said, given that she was very tuned into the present moment and nothing escaped her attention.

Janice had been initiated as a Native American ceremonialist and also practiced a form of Mongolian shamanism, which includes extraction and soul retrieval work. Born and raised in New York City in a Jewish family, Janice had been ill as a child. This illness helped turn her attention to natural forms of healing, which she then became acquainted with and would go on to utilize in her healing work.

She was very grateful to be invited to a Sundance ceremony on the Pine Ridge reservation in South Dakota, feeling strongly that she was guided there. It was here that Janice had one of her very powerful visions. She is a keeper of a sacred Native American pipe and an Inipi ceremonial lodge (sweat lodge), and she has been a Sun-Dancer for almost a decade.

Janice explained to me from the start, the type of work she performed and, to be honest, I never found any of what she said strange at all. Being an Irish Catholic from West Belfast I had never heard of such practices or anything else about these various healing modalities that these healers regularly employed. However, it's amazing how desperation and pain will open your mind to different methods of healing that might otherwise sound outlandish. The word *shaman* means "one who sees in the dark." The question is, What exactly do they see? Where do they go and what do they see? In my first conversation with Janice she explained what she would try to do for me, and went on to inform me that there are three worlds in which a shaman travels: the lower world, the middle world, and the upper world. All three worlds are filled with spirits that become helpers in the healing process. It's amazing how I began to have faith in this language and healing processes. I was to learn that having faith in a modality that one is using contributes to one's healing in a major way, whether it's the 12 steps or shamanism.

I later learned through journeying that the lower world has spirit helpers in animal form; the middle world has a wide variety of different spirits; and the upper world has spirit helpers in human form. Later on down the line I got to experience what it was like in these worlds with some of these spirits myself when I was invited to journey.

It was explained to me that we are surrounded by helping spirits, but when we are vulnerable or low on energy, they are at a remove from us and we don't have a lot of protection from darker entities or energies that exist. (This seemed to be a steady baseline theme from all the healers I worked with.) Shamanism is one of the oldest healing practices on the planet. In ancient tribes and villages everyone lived together and played their part. The elders were taken care of, the tribe raised the children, and every tribe had a medicine man or shaman. If a child had a traumatic experience of any sort, such as suffering a bad fall or being attacked by a wild animal, the child would be brought to the shaman within a matter of days and a soul retrieval would be performed on the child (by the shaman).

When trauma strikes a human being, the soul sometimes can't deal with the pain that's involved. As a defense mechanism of sorts, that part of the soul then fragments and a piece of the person's true essence falls away. In other words, they lose a part of themselves. The shaman performs a ceremony with continuous drumbeats and rattles to induce an altered state of consciousness in themselves and the person being healed. The shaman then journeys into the spirit world with information about the ill client, and gives it to the spirits who then retrieve the fragmented soul part. The spirit helpers pass the missing piece along to the shaman who then, acting as a messenger between both the spirit world and the physical realm, places the fragmented piece back into the human being's essence. After an integration period, a sense of wholeness is then achieved and experienced by the individual undergoing the shamanic healing.

This can be an exhausting process for both the shaman and the client. The indigenous people didn't have the same problems that our society is plagued by today, such as depression, anxiety, and addiction. Or perhaps I should say, maybe these issues existed but not to the extent that they do now. I have learned the hard way that numbing oneself with different medications that are readily available from most doctors these days is not a permanent solution to these ailments and causes more trouble in the long run. I'm not implying that this is gospel or that certain folks don't need to be medicated, but from my own experiences and the experience I've had in working with others, most people don't actually need to take any kind of antidepressant drugs. I have found they just aren't willing to "man up" and take the steps necessary to find a spiritual solution to what's generally a spiritual problem. Doing so may mean enduring a certain level of discomfort and typically the doctor's prescription always seems like an easier way out.

* * *

That sunny September day I left the job site early and set off downtown to Janice's office in Chelsea in lower Manhattan. I was really nervous and I recall my whole system being totally out of balance. Part of me, however, was relieved that I was taking action and trying my hardest to find healing; what more can a person do? I knew that Janice was authentic and could help me in some way even though she had told me at the start that she couldn't make any promises. I liked that she was a straight shooter, unlike some of the creeps I would meet down the line. She helped me to believe in what I was doing and said that was a huge part of healing. Most people don't get well because of their own negative thinking; apparently, in part, it's a manifestation thing.

I got some water and approached the entrance to Janice's apartment building. It was all very plush, with Janice's name on the front door alongside other names with letters beside them. From the moment the doorman told me to go down the hallway and to the left I could smell the sage burning. I rang her buzzer and a very bubbly lady in her late fifties, with beautiful blonde hair, answered the door.

"Hi, Adrian," Janice said in her piercing voice. "How are you?" She invited me in and sat me down; there were Native American symbols all over the room, as well as different eagle feathers and many instruments: a wide variety of rattles and a few different size drums. It was obvious to me that this stuff hadn't been bought on the Internet. It was all authentic, having been handcrafted by skilled tradespeople on different reservations and from all corners of the globe. There were multicolored blankets and an array of what I assumed to be shamanic symbols and healing instruments in this up market Chelsea abode.

Here with Janice, I found myself lying on her table, blindfolded, and with what appeared to be a bearskin over me. A recording consisting of constant drumming drummed out at me through a speaker, accompanied by Janice drumming on her own personal drum. She told me to relax as she blindfolded herself with a scarlet, red-colored scarf. Between the drumbeats and the strong scent of sage I fell within myself and tried to lay still under the chatter of my screaming mind as the healing ceremony began.

Really fast consistent drumbeats bring a person into an altered state of consciousness, which creates an opening for everything that needs to take place. I would hear the shaman chant out strange noises; the whole session must have lasted ninety minutes. Janice brought everything she had to the table; it was calming and very moving to be a part of it. Toward the end of the ceremony she put her mouth and lips on the crown of my head and blew really hard into it and then repeated the same actions in my solar plexus region.

When the ceremony was over I could hear her say my name in a very subtle voice, asking me how I was doing. She removed the cover from my eyes and said, "Wow!" and proceeded to tell me that a lot had happened in the journey that she had taken. Janice has a rule that she never discusses past events from people's lives that they themselves aren't aware of, especially if they were traumatic, dark experiences. She had captured some of these happenings on the soul retrieval journey she had undertaken on my behalf but she refused to discuss them with me as she believed that they can cause even more trouble when the ego attaches itself to those past experiences. She did, however, discuss with me some of the other visions she had experienced in the healing as we sat on the floor wrapping prayers and burning tobacco as an offering to the spirit guides that had participated in the session.

The shaman explained that she seen me in a previous life, on horseback, returning from a hunt dragging a dead animal and bringing it to a tent where I talked with what appeared to be a Native American chief with very elaborate headwear on. The medicine man from that tribe had shown up in my healing session, together with other significant symbols, spirits, and healers.

Before I left the apartment to head back out into the busy New York hustle, Janice explained to me that everything for me was now about integration and letting the experience of the day blend into my life.

I would go on to have many sessions with Janice wherein she would perform many extractions on me. She brought much spiritual power back to me through soul retrieval and power animal retrieval. She made a great contribution to my overall healing and I have remained friends with her, as she is a quality person to have beside me on this journey of life.

Abdi Assadi was the third healer I worked with initially. He's another truly gifted healer with an amazing insight into realms that are unknown to most. He became a lighthouse in the stormiest waters of my life, a real guardian angel. I emailed him frequently when I was completely terrified and the wisdom and depth of his replies were inspiring. It was comforting to know that he understood my situation. As I passed through one fit of madness after another, our email interactions kept me going; there was never a time that I didn't get a reply. Our cyber correspondence was comprised of a very strange language from what I was used to, but I was learning. I had to, for my life depended on it. I think doctors would have wanted to lock us up if they had listened to our conversations—but what do doctors really know at the end of the day, other than what they've been taught in some school?

A year after I'd first made contact with Abdi, I actually got to meet him in person at his office in Manhattan. He was the first person in my whole ordeal to actually tell me that I was waking up, and that resulted in my beginning to frame my process in a context of awakening. I still continue to see Abdi today for guidance or when I have something I want to run past him, or just to have my energy checked and cleaned up from time to time.

* * *

Despite the help I was getting from these wonderful healers, my mental obsessions remained unbearable at times. I frequently believed that I would crash and burn, and not make it through these intense cycles running through me. What seemed like a serious issue or problem would seemingly come out of nowhere. The effect this would have on my body was one of trauma, which would torment me and drive me crazy for days at a time. I would feel as if I was hanging on for dear life as fears flooded through me and overwhelmed me.

One of my main fears was that if this continued I wouldn't be able to function and I'd end up homeless on the street. As well, the fear about alcohol was still surfacing amidst the other bundles of fear that raced around my brain. As thoughts rushed in and out I got a sense that some sort of death or elimination was occurring but I couldn't be sure about that, given that it was happening at an alarming speed and it seemed like it would never end. Typically the cycle of thoughts would run its course and then I would be blessed with a grace period of calmness and serenity. This resting period was new to my experience and sometimes it felt like absolute bliss. As this continued, I began to get a stronger sense that something was happening through me, for it was becoming clearer that the energy was cleansing my system. It appeared to be dislodging and releasing old emotional junk—stuff that I had been weighed down with for decades and, as I'd been told, from previous lifetimes.

Many old events from my past that were etched into and stored in my energetic field were being set free, and this wasn't a pleasant process. Unhappy scenes from when I was a kid would shoot into my memory—sometimes stuff I had long forgotten. Flashbacks from different, painful parts of my life were coming to the surface at an alarming rate. Everything from drunken arguments with my ex-girlfriend, the teacher screaming in my face as a child to fighting with the British Army in the street in Belfast was coming forth. Most of it was dark negative material, which makes sense today as I know for sure it was a cleansing taking place. But back then, experiencing it all over again in all its original intensity was no fun. The experiences were being dredged up from as far back as I could remember, alongside other thoughts and intuitions I had no recollection of at all.

Added to this was the fact that there weren't any rules—no guidelines to follow. Penney had told me that the energy, once it was processed, would leave through weak points in my body and mind. It certainly felt like it was making my back injury worse. This was part of the aftermath of the "physic surgery" that had been performed by the Whisperer. I was also in an awakening process. They are both part of each other, really. They were for me, anyway. I've been told by various folks that most people who awaken, awaken more subtly over time. However, I know it can happen in many different ways. Mine just happened to come at me like a freight train shooting through my being over and over again, and it had all the flashes, lights, and visuals to go right along with it.

I sometimes listen to people in recovery circles say things like "I wish I could have a white light experience or some sort of thunderous experience." I would reply to them, "Be careful what you ask for as it might not be what you want and you won't ever be able to reverse it. And if you're like me you sure as hell might not be able to handle it." I've also heard cases of people not making it through some of these energetic upheavals because they are just too powerful. But if the truth be told, most people either don't want to awaken or don't even know that they have the capacity to do so—they are too attached to and identified with "things."

In any event, my soul had been cracked open and much activity was emerging from it. This was really the Divine at work in me and I could sense that underneath everything at times. Healing was going to take time, as well as guidance from the right people, but they *were* showing up for me in the midst of my intense spiritual conundrum.

I believe that where there is darkness there is also light—one can't exist without the other. The beautiful reality was that every turn I found a life preserver just when I needed it most, through the right person, the right book, or an inspirational email—or even a friend cooking dinner for me or inviting me on a fishing trip. There was a catalogue of miracles that were personal to me that helped me keep the faith and gave me the strength to keep on the path. Because of where I have been and what I have emerged from, I have come to know that anything is possible.

* * *

I continued along on my journey, struggling every step of the way, but I was moving and something seemed like it was unfolding. To me it felt as if a "super life-force energy" was in control of my nervous system and my entire body. The exorcism didn't seem to have any value or power to me anymore and it became really clear to me that that experience was over, even though I would still become a little obsessed with it from time to time.

I was about to embark on the most amazing discovery about myself, my condition, and what was occurring within me—just when I thought it couldn't take any more twists and turns on the rocky road that I called my life.

Chapter 8
On the Ropes at Work

I was a single guy who lived alone with no one to take care of me, and even though I had been in the States for a while and was a citizen, America was still a foreign country. I didn't have any family around to keep an eye on me, so I had to work to keep the wolves away from the door, simple as that. I had been out of work for almost one year since my injury at the power plant. It's hard to survive in a city like New York for long without bringing home a weekly paycheck. And besides, the embodied spirit of the Irish immigrant was alive and well within me—that drive to continue working and making my living was still very much present.

I was really hurting financially, right down to my last dollars, and I needed a job, even though I wasn't fit enough to return to my old line of work. I was plagued by waves of crippling fatigue and the energy would hurt my body so much I would lie on my bed for days at a time. I was spacing out quite a bit and I couldn't hold my attention on anything for very long as the energetic movements shuffling through me were incredibly distracting. The fearful thoughts were still very much my companion as well.

* * *

One Monday morning at 4:00 a.m. I decided to get out of bed. It was a hot and humid August morning in New York. I got my tools together and drove to my union hall, which was on 10th Avenue on the West Side. Normally I would have taken the train there but I honestly couldn't walk that far to the train station the way my legs were.

What a godsend it was to be part of a great union in New York City! I went down the stairs and entered my details into the phone system at the hiring hall. Within a couple of minutes the business agent came out of his office and shouted my name. He asked me whether or not I had my welding license with me. I told him I did. We chatted for a bit, just some small talk, before he asked me if I could pass a drug test on the job site. He then proceeded to give me a piece of paper on which was written the phone number of the job's shop steward.

He told me to go out to Aqueduct Racetrack in Queens because they were building a new casino there. It was a really big job that would have a lot of overtime. This wasn't necessarily a good thing as far as I was concerned because I was worried about trying to complete a regular eight-hour day instead of the twelve hours they were putting in daily. In any event, he meant well, so I thanked him and headed out in my car. In some respects I felt happy that I was going back to work but I was also very concerned and afraid at the same time as everything in my life had changed and I was about to find out just how much.

I passed the drug test and started to work on the job as a welder, even though I was struggling to get into the swing of things. I practically forced myself to go to work every morning. I would get out of bed at 4:30 a.m. after not having had much sleep, and make my way to the job to try to make a living. My father had one of the best work ethics I had ever known. He had a brother nicknamed "Lazy Tom" who had humorously gotten that name because he was an incredibly hard worker. I inherited that quality and besides, I have never seen too many lazy Irishmen on the job.

At work, my mind would do a number on me all day long, for most of my cohorts projected a deep sense of negativity. I could feel this most acutely and it made me nauseous. I sensed what issues they carried and could see the different fears and situations they had in their lives. It was intense. Looking at someone's face and seeing the characteristics of his or her soul had been something that had just switched on in me—it had appeared one day completely out of the blue.

The body is like an energetic grid with different energy centers and sensors. Mine felt like they were wide open with no filters and picking up everything around me. All of me and all of life seemed like it was underneath a huge magnifying glass. Everything I could hear and feel was sharp and loud—and everything I laid eyes on was very bright and incredibly amplified. I was treading carefully so as not to react to everything that was happening around me, for my nerves were completely on edge. On top of this, the work was really difficult and I shouldn't have been there at all in my state, but defiantly I persevered because of the financial bind I was in.

This all-knowing capacity is what is called clairvoyance in spiritual circles but I wasn't to find that out until later. In the beginning I didn't know what to do with all the information I was picking up and it overwhelmed me; I knew other people weren't living from this place, experiencing what I was experiencing. I certainly wasn't used to living my life in this way.

* * *

I knew some of the guys on this job from previous jobs I had been on and I also made new friends. I liked my partner also as he dug in and we worked well together. However, I could see a whole bunch of shit going on with this company that I didn't really care for, especially as regards how some of the workers were being unfairly treated.

I decided that I was going to keep my mouth shut given that this was my first job back. I am good union man, and I love how the unions have been set up to protect honest hardworking people from greedy, corrupt corporations. That said, I hate to see the working man being mistreated and I equally dislike watching workers take advantage of the company by trying to take liberties. I think this stems from my upbringing and what I'd observed in Belfast with what the uninvited British authorities did in my country. Besides, my father had been in the Seaman's Union and had also been a shop steward on his job. I have never liked bullies!

We were working for an out-of-town outfit and their superintendent seemed quite mouthy with a lot of the men. He was also pulling some moves that my union delegate wouldn't have appreciated. I had a gut feeling that the superintendent and I would eventually cross paths but I was trying to stay away from him. I just wanted to do my job and go home. The long hours were taking their toll on me: twelve-hour days, seven days a week. I was totally exhausted and pushing it to the max. One of the problems with working these longs shifts was that everyone would get cranky and be on edge, and sometimes arguments would flare up over nothing.

On this particular Sunday I had been on this job for just over a month. I was welding in a stairwell and the cranky superintendent came by and started running his mouth off at me and my partner. A combination of thoughts and rage started to run through me; I could feel it had been building up for a while with this boy. I jumped to my feet, shouting and screaming at him, asking him how dare he come from Philadelphia and talk to me like that—or to any New York ironworker for that matter. I could see in his beady little eyes that he was frightened and shitting his pants. The last place he wanted to be in that moment was on that stairwell with me in this mood—I got a bit of a kick out of that.

My partner was super surprised but I could tell he was happy and enjoyed watching me giving it to this guy. I knew I had lost my job. My partner had already told me that if I was fired then he was going also. I came really close to beating the balls out of the superintendent but something stopped me from following through. My partner and I had a good laugh about it as I walked off the job but underneath it all I was concerned with how easily I had flipped out; my temper had been very bad back in my drinking days. Was I returning to that combative type of behavior? I sincerely hoped not; even though I had my moments in recovery, I had mellowed out quite a bit.

I didn't even bother going to work the next morning and awoke to my phone ringing. The shop steward was on the other end and it didn't take a rocket scientist to figure out what he was calling me for. I told him I would stop by to collect my check. On the way I called my union delegate and he'd been briefed on everything already. He was cool and even sang my praises a little bit and agreed this guy was a scoundrel. Then he gave me another job. (You've got to love being part of a great union; getting fired then being sent back to work the next day!) The union took care of me as long as I didn't abuse it, which I never had—I'm very grateful for it.

The next morning I started over in the Brooklyn Navy Yard with my new company. After being there for a few days they found out I could weld and asked if I would go to a job in Long Island City where a welder was needed. I declined the offer as two welders there had already been fired; their welds weren't passing inspection. The job seemed like pressure and unwanted attention I could do without. I was trying desperately to keep a low profile and stay away from stressful situations.

However, the boss worked me over for a while and made me an offer I couldn't refuse, so I agreed. As it turned out it was great because they gave me extra money when they saw that my welds passed inspection. I was also happy that this job was only ten minutes away from my house. I got to weld all day under my shield, just me and my thoughts all day long—they were intense and cyclic. Every once in a while the guy that was doing fire watch for me would check in to see if I needed anything.

Occasionally I would notice that my internal situation had shifted a little bit and had gotten a little softer. It was still at such an extreme level—but I could pick up even the slightest change. According to Abdi, this whole thing was a process. This made sense, for again, I had the strongest intuition that the crazy thoughts were a detoxification; the old programmed conditioning was exiting and it didn't feel good at all. All the racing thoughts and intense energetic movements in my body were nothing but this mysterious intelligent cleansing cycle in full swing.

I had been emailing Abdi for months at this point. He had

answered a lot of my questions, especially on issues like this. His guidance was golden and it enabled me to continue to keep a low profile and try to just do my work every day. It felt reassuring to be told one more time on the phone that I was in the midst of a process and it was taking place through me and to stop taking it so personally. And again on the phone he reminded me that entity removal was just the beginning; the more traumatic part was the process that follows. I told him I couldn't get my head around all that had happened. He replied by saying that my only chance would be for me to get my heart around it and forget about getting my head around it—that I couldn't ever understand such an experience intellectually.

He assured me that it was a good idea to not repeat our conversations to anyone, for most folks wouldn't understand it at all. And when I asked him "Why me?" I was not expecting the response I got.

"Why not?" he wanted to know. He told me about parts of his own experience. He had lived with things randomly moving around his apartment for an entire year before he ended up in hospital bleeding. His point was that he had been through significant stuff also but he had made it through. Now he could help me. So why not? He reminded me that I had gone through so much misery when drinking and using drugs and I had made it through that. This was a good point. He also said that when he read my first email he knew that my soul had signed up for this whole journey. Abdi went on to say that both our souls were laughing at the conversation our personalities were having.

I explained that every time I would run into difficulties and it seemed that there was no way out, a major lifeline would present itself. He agreed and went on to tell me that there is a greater power in charge of it all and it was holding me up. I asked him about the spiritual path and what I should be doing.

Were there any teachers I could see? He told me not to worry about the teachers. Instead he told me to sit with myself in meditation for five minutes every day. He gave me a very simple practice to use, basically just sitting with myself and the energies without trying to figure it all out. He told me that meditation could really help stabilize me when I was in choppy waters. I talked to him about the obsessive thoughts, as they were still very concerning at times. Abdi said they were attachments related to everything that had happened to me, and as such, that they were part of the detox process of my mind and soul.

This is what I had earnestly suspected. I certainly wasn't hearing it in the recovery circles I was running in. In fact, to recovery circles, obsession is seen as negative and dangerous. For people in recovery, it can be a threat to go back to old ways. Generally when someone has obsessive thoughts around booze or drugs, they are being reeled back into that vice or behavior again. My experience was proving to be something completely different. The obsessions I was experiencing were a fuel in which karma was being burnt off and escorted from my psyche. This was all very traumatic and confusing to a person like myself who had never fathomed such happenings.

As time went on I would learn that these obsessive thoughts were by-products of old rage and anger that had been living deep down inside of my soul for a very long time. I didn't even bother trying to explain this to people that were close to me, for I knew that I would receive strange looks.

The spiritual work that I'd done had helped keep me afloat and I can see I had awakened enough spiritually to see a shift taking place inside of me. This enabled me to see the world from different eyes. I was really blessed that I didn't return to my old ways and that I didn't give in to any of the crazy thoughts that sometimes still ran through my brain. As Abdi had mentioned, I was safe and protected and that's why I remained unharmed or unfazed by the thoughts of taking up the booze again, as scary as they were.

He also told me that there was a reason all this was happening to me. He reminded me that I was now as open as I had ever been and this would enable me to help people. He felt confident that in a few years people undergoing experiences similar to mine would be coming to me for guidance. As you might imagine, everything he told me was incredibly reassuring to hear, and all of it has turned out to be true.

* * *

I would continue to try to go to work every day, even though it was difficult to stay in the moment, perform as a welder, and climb around on a building. In any event, every day that I could work I considered a great blessing and was grateful for this bonus.

It was Saturday, October 29, and I had an appointment with Penney at her place. I always looked forward to seeing her for I knew that she had great power and I never knew what was going to take place. I had never seen the likes of her healing work before. On this particular day she would display some of her greatest gifts in a way that was completely authentic without being showy.

Typically she would look all over my body and touch it with the palms of her hands, like a healer who was joined as one with her work. Then she would say to me, "Spit on my hand, don't worry about it, just do it," as she was pulling stuff up out of me. I'd watch this lady closely as she puffed and panted and breathed deeply. Sweat would appear on her forehead and drip from her brow—it always appeared to be such hard work for her and as she worked she would continue to make little comments, half out of breath.

I was always aware that there were more things taking place between her and me than would appear to be the case on a physical level. I also more or less understood why she would tell me to shut up at times: It looked like she was taking on all the energy that was coming up in me and it was grueling hard work by the looks of things. Invariably something darker, heavier, or more intense would arise and give her a tough time. At other moments, Penney would laugh and comment when she saw comical images appear from my aura. She would channel these energies through herself, almost like a human with a magnetic power.

Often she would see stuff from my past and comment on it and even sprinkle something about the future into the mix as she gazed into my body. Typically, she was having a whole different experience from the session than I was.

I would joke with her at times and say things like, "I want to be a healer like you—can I be your apprentice? Or go to healer school?" as I lay on her table. At this she would reply, "Where do you think you are now, baby?" and we would both smile.

Looking back I realize that she knew way more about my life and what was coming up than she could ever reveal to me. I believe that, for my own protection, she didn't share a lot of the information she was getting. Oh, she sometimes gave me glimpses of it—that was candy for my ego back then. But anything she told me would invariably start the question machine up—the need to know everything—rolling in my head again. This creates fear, and that's harmful to the healing process. This need to know on my part faded out over time, for things came to the point that I really *didn't* need to know—it didn't really matter to me anymore.

On this particular day Penney was working on me and she began to tell me that I was going to hold a really good position with a really big company and make a lot of money. The work would involve putting the "skin" on high-rise buildings. She gave me what she was seeing in great detail and as it turned out, she was pretty accurate with her information. Down the line I actually became a foreman for one of the biggest curtain wall companies in the country. Curtain wall are large panels made from metal and glass; they are referred to as "the skin" around a building. From a financial standpoint, I also had my best financial year that year, just like she said I would.

As I lay on her table on this Saturday afternoon she told me to be really careful with a steel beam on the job. This startled me and I told her, "You need to be clearer than that—what the fuck are you talking about—please don't half tell me about this, you have me afraid."

But all she would say was, "Don't worry, sweetie pie."

I hassled her to tell me what she meant by the steel beam comment, because I was working with really big steel I-beams at work. I felt scared when she told me I was going to take a tumble but would be fine. My ego went into overdrive and was having a right go at trying to forecast what this tumble would look like— but somehow I then totally forget all about what she had said.

* * *

In work on Monday I just went about my business and wasn't on guard at all—I had totally forgotten my session with Penney. I took all the equipment out of the gang box and set up for work, got on my scaffold, and started welding a stiffener onto a steel beam. As I was working on the detail, the fully extended scaffold got shaky and then flipped over. I tried to grab onto the steel beam but I couldn't hang on because I had big thick leather welding gloves on my hands. I went down about twelve feet and landed on my back. As I went down, the grinder switched on and just missed my face. I felt the thud; I was really banged up and in shock.

Luckily, I got out of the way and got the grinder on the leg instead of the face. As I was lying on the floor beside the scaffold my coworkers came running to my aid. The first thing I remembered was my conversation with Penney.

As I got my bearings I could feel the adrenaline rush through my body. My coworkers sat me down and tried to get me to chill out. I went for a walk down by where the welding machines were situated to clear my head and scan my body for damages. My phone rang—it was Penney. Alarmed and connecting everything together I started blurting out what had just happened. She just said, "Don't be worrying, you're going to be fine."

The next day I missed work due to a sharp pain in my back. I knew I had done damage in the fall, but the more serious repercussions from it weren't to come until a few months later in February. It's easy to look back and see quite clearly that the universe was trying to get my attention by telling me to get out of this job. However, I wasn't listening, for I had way too much fear going on to take that step. After all, this was my livelihood.

I have since learned the hard way that the truth will always keep rapping at the door until you eventually sit up and pay attention to it. Whether it's a toxic relationship you won't leave and continue to tell yourself lies about to sooth the fears or your relationship with money, food, or alcohol—or in my case this job—the universe will get in your face and force you to make a move to give it up. If you don't, it might eventually kill you. I had to awaken more and burn a lot more karma—and basically get sick and tired of going against my soul's desire every day—and then eventually get injured again down the line—before I would learn this lesson.

Stubbornly I continued to work; I had missed so much time already. I was in six figures of debt, partly due to some bad advice from an accountant about some investments I had made. For the next few months I showed up to work every day for an iron outfit. I recall this period, for I suffered from chronic insomnia at night, during which time I would have the terrors. However, when I did sleep I would have insane nightmares. This was clearly a no-win situation.

As time went on, the physical pain in my neck and back became very difficult to deal with. I was aware that I had two injuries but it was very obvious that the physical pain was also emerging from a lot of the paranormal activity and energy that was coursing through my body; it couldn't be ignored or denied. When the energy and activity became so much in my body, I would escape into my head and get stuck in there for hours. The energy would rush through me like it was taking me over, like 540 voltage going through a 120-watt system. I sensed that the energy was running in intelligent cycles given that I could feel different parts of my body being worked on; it was like it was being rewired or reformed. Another analogy would be that it felt like the actions of a sewing machine restitching each part of my body and its DNA. In individual pieces it would do its work then move to the next bit, after spending days and sometimes weeks on one part.

Whatever part it connected to experienced a sensation that was akin to electric-like maggots eating their way through that body part. Sometimes it would be my left calf muscle, then it would move to a position on my neck. At other times my neck would pop right out of shape and I would be in intense pain for days.

I later learned that this action is called *kriya* in spiritual circles (in Sanskrit). Kriya refers to outward physical expression of awakened Kundalini energy and can present as spontaneous yoga postures. I wouldn't be able to move and almost cried at times with the pain. As the energy rushed to my brain I would be disoriented and debilitated and I would completely lose my memory, sometimes for seconds and other times much longer. I would experience chronic migraines, for I could feel the plates in my head rotate when this intelligent life-force went to work on the rewiring of my brain. The majority of the time I hadn't a clue what was occurring. I can still feel the energy and the spasms some days but thank heavens I now know what it is and the energy is definitely flowing with more continuity.

I would watch moments of my life flash through my mind's eye as if they were being replayed on a video screen. This was very distracting and overwhelming at work, where I would hide behind my welding screen and try to pay attention to what I was doing while the mayhem was unfolding. I would have given anything to be rid of the fatigue that was seriously handicapping me and preventing me from moving around. It was like my life and body weren't my own anymore; this force had an agenda and it was going to have its way with me no matter what my ego said about it, or how much resistance I put up. At times the self-centered, raging movie that played in my head would rip through my mind at what seemed like 100 MPH as it was joined by the wind howling through my system with all kinds of illusory entities. I would yell "FUCKING STOP, please! For heaven's sake, I can't take it anymore!" It would be relentless. Totally clueless to what was happening, at times I would feel like I was falling to pieces. I had a very pale complexion and my work mates would ask me if I was okay.

I worked for four months on the iron everyday but the accident would come back to haunt me. It was February by now and right in the midst of another New York winter, the pains in my neck became ever more serious. My neck and shoulder locked in all sorts of strange positions that left me on my bed in agony. I could no longer even carry the welding lead in work anymore, I ached so badly. My partner at work told me I needed to go see a doctor but the fear factor of being out of work again prevented me from doing so.

I was under a lot of stress about my finances, along with everything else that was happening. On Presidents Day weekend I awoke to an unbearable pain. My neck was locked and I found it very difficult to move around. My friend got me to a doctor and after an examination and some X-rays she started some chiropractic treatment to manipulate my neck back into place. The X-rays had shown that my shoulder's left side was out of alignment with the right side by almost three inches as a result of the pain shooting from my neck.

I started to visit this doctor four times each week.

I was to spend the next nine months on the bench again and out of work.

I'd be out in the supermarket and my neck would lock into a strange position and my body would fill with an amazing energy that would almost take my breath away. I didn't have much to go on except that this was some sort of cleanse that was connected to a spiritual process, that's what I prayed for, anyway. I didn't have a say in the process or the outcome——talk about feeling powerless.

The bright lights, my life flashing in front of me, the physical pain and fatigue, rage, the hot and cold surges that would speed up and down my spine, the visions and noises, the faces of people, the insane mood swings—I found it impossible to hold it all together at times. I had all kinds of hunches and ideas about my condition but of course when in the eye of a storm like this, nothing can be figured out. On top of that, I really didn't have anyone to process this stuff with. Penney didn't like discussing it as that wasn't part of her work and when I tried to she would let me know we couldn't talk about it as it would affect my healing. Abdi obviously wasn't available every day.

When it would get really bad I would talk to some folks in my recovery circle and sometimes I would be in a worse way after that. They didn't get it and, looking back, it was crazy of me to think they even should. Although I have to say my recovery mentor Bob gave me so much phone time and really worked hard with me to find answers. I was blessed to have him.

I spent most of my time at home alone, trying to endure the onslaught and process as best I could. Today it's obvious to me that life wanted me out of the environment of that job. It was too loud, rough, and aggressive for the open energetic field that my body had become. My central nervous system and body were in desperate need of integration and healing with my soul and I didn't fully understand that. I was so sensitive that if I nipped my finger or banged it with a hammer it was much more painful than what it would normally have been.

It seemed so cruel to be removed from work. I had to believe that this was God's compassion and grace, giving me time away to let this experience unfold. When I look back on it all, the real cruelty was that the ego was trying to keep me at work, suffering every day. I was such a stubborn Irishman who wouldn't surrender, for I was born and raised believing surrender is for the weak. So after being eight months out of work and in pain, I returned to the union hall looking for another job to go back yet again.

I wasn't able to work by a long shot but I was willing to force my will to give it another try. However, not much good comes out of forcing life. That old self with those same old fears would hang in there, telling me that I wouldn't survive without this job, that it was too tall an order to trust that the Divine was taking care of me. That old self told me I would end up on the street under a bridge, eating out of dumpsters.

I wasn't willing to relinquish my desire to go back to work

for a long time. In fact, it would almost kill me before I would give up the fight and loosen my grip. I started to feel paranoid going back to the union hall so often, which was out of character for me. I had never had to do this; I had always held my own out there. My getting hurt made it look like there was drama and I was some sort of problematic guy that I never had been. I had always been in the union's good graces.

It was hard to just walk away from a big salary and all the benefits that came with a good career. Where would I go?

* * *

I met my friend Joe on the way to the union hall on what was a wet October morning, just by chance—if you can believe that anything happens just by chance. I encountered him on a side street on the West Side of Manhattan at 5:00 a.m. and there he was. He asked me where I had been, and said that he hadn't run into me out in the field for quite some time. I explained that I'd had a few injuries on the job. I wasn't gullible enough to explain what else was going on with me in the paranormal realm. Turns out that the work injuries were a great disguise; actually they were a great cover in many ways through my entire journey.

Even though Joe was a great guy I couldn't tell him about all the internal shit that I had been going through. He told me that he was the shop steward at the World Trade Center and he would love me to come onto his job to work. He said that it might take a few weeks to get matters all sorted out but he would definitely get me on it if I wanted the gig. I took some information from him and immediately began the process of getting my security clearance. In the meantime I got a welding job to keep me ticking over.

The stress and the anxiety of trying to show up every day and deal with the characters at work was unbearable at times. The construction industry is loaded with drug addicts and alcoholics who are tough to be around. It's a dog-eat-dog industry at times and some people will stab you in the back while they invite you out to lunch. I was always watching my back on that job, which added to my stress—but you did meet the good guys also.

* * *

It was a strange energy at the World Trade Center site—no surprises after everything that had happened there on 9/11. I remembered my visit with the Horse Whisperer back in Ireland, and what he had told me about the strange reports from people he had talked to who had been there. I remembered that he said to "be careful." It was ironic that I was to end up working there after the conversation I'd had with him, making me believe that everything really might be connected after all.

To my surprise, I could feel a nice peaceful energy in the air on that job. I remember bringing this to my partner's attention one day as I took in the energy. Outside on the street it was a very different story, with all the hustle and bustle from nosey tourists taking pictures beside the bankers who were heading into their towers of finance. That created a different vibe that would almost choke me at times and make me feel dizzy—it was a dark, greed-filled vibe.

I was very honored to work on that job, replacing the twin towers, with my ironworker union brothers. It was more than just a job; to me it symbolized evolution and a great healing in many ways. Hopefully the families who had lost love ones there felt some healing also. This job had a lot of overtime and I worked Saturdays and Sundays and late most nights, which was a real turning point for me because I was able to get out of the debt I was in. I even began to save some money.

Eventually the work came to an end and I was ready to take some time off to relax and rest up as my body was fried from all the job-related stress. But the shop steward wouldn't hear tell of it. He told me that the business agent wanted to send me to another job. I couldn't get out of it and ended up at Madison Square Garden the next day as a welder, getting the place ready for the hockey season. This was another seven-day-a-week job.

Normally, I would have been gratified but it was like a slow torture and my condition wasn't improving at all.

It was mid-July and the heat with the work was grueling but I continued to get out of bed every day and kept it all going. I recall sitting outside Madison Square Garden in the mornings, in a state of distress in the blistering heat, wondering to myself how I could roust myself from the sidewalk and walk in there, let alone make it through another twelve-hour day. The whole journey had been tough, but around this time it was like lightning was running through me all day long. The picture on my security pass from that job says it all; I look frantic in it. I was about to find out what was really wrong with me and get some serious answers as to why my condition persisted.

Chapter 9
The Ego in Its Death Throes

One day my friend Bill called me up and said he and his girlfriend wanted to visit me. At my apartment a few hours later, he asked me what was up with me. I tried explaining to him what was happening. His reply was another defining moment, for he mentioned a word that would change my life in so many ways. It was a word that I could only ever recall having heard once before.

My friend said it sounded like "Kundalini" energy was coursing through me. The word *Kundalini* came out of his mouth and pierced deep into my soul, and all of a sudden I couldn't think about anything but this word. I began to do a Google search on it and was totally amazed by what I started to uncover.

As I scrolled through the search results that came up on my computer screen, material about Kundalini energy and Kundalini awakening appeared everywhere. But let me make one thing clear from the start—when I talk of Kundalini, I don't mean it in the context of Kundalini yoga. Instead, the Kundalini I refer to is an awakening of an intelligent mechanism in the body, responsible for making the process of spiritual awakening itself occur.

If you mention the word *Kundalini* these days in the West, a lot of people assume you mean Kundalini yoga. Practicing Kundalini yoga and having a Kundalini awakening are entirely different things. Kundalini yoga may lead to Kundalini energy being activated in a person but that is a rarity, especially in the West. The majority of Kundalini yoga teachers certainly do not have awakened Kundalini, as I have found from personal interaction with quite a few of them.

The country where Kundalini emerged is generally attributed to what today is known as India, where it prevailed in various practices and traditions. References to Kundalini are found in the teachings of the East Indian Hindu religious texts known as the Upanishads, which date from roughly 4000 to 5000 BCE. The Upanishads are considered part of the Hindu scriptures, specifically the Vedic texts or Vedas. These poetic texts, possibly dating from as far back as 1500 BCE and perhaps thousands of years earlier, delve into such matters as philosophy, meditation, and the true nature of God.

In ancient times it seems that Kundalini awakening was much more connected to yoga practices than it is in today's spiritual materialized Western yoga practices. Kundalini yoga in today's Western world is very rarely accompanied with Kundalini activation. That said, I know of cases where it has happened but they seem to be few and far between. Most people that seek out this energy very rarely ever come in contact with it.

Coiled Kundalini is symbolized by a serpent at rest, positioned in the form of a coil. The Sanskrit word *Kundal,* which means "spiral" or "coil," is the basis of the word *Kundalini.* Indeed, *Kundalini Shakti* means "coiled power," and in the ancient classic Indian texts there are many references to it. In the work Shankaracharya, Saurya Ladarius, says: "The invincible Kundalini Shakti, pierces the chakras and enters its abode step by step," and in the Mundamalatantra Kundalini it is referred to as "the basic force of the body." It is called "the supreme power" in the Varahopanished.

Basically Kundalini is a primordial cosmic life-force that resides at the base of the spine in all human beings, but most often it lays there asleep and inactivated. In ancient scriptures it is deemed to be, as mentioned above, a serpent that is coiled three and a half times; it is known as "the serpent energy." As it activates, uncoils, and rises up the spine through the subtle channels of the central nervous system, it works its way through the body's energy centers (chakras) and through the crown chakra to bring about communion with the Divine and sometimes enlightenment in the human being. As the energy rushes to the brain it transforms the brain chemistry and brings about a DNA upgrade within the person who has activated the Kundalini energy, burning off anything that's not pure within the human structure. In so doing, all the old karmic junk that one carries is brought to the surface of life for processing and purification, which leads to higher states of consciousness. All of one's old emotional sludge that's ingrained in the energy field and mind—that muck gets scraped off of the soul.

That said, there are different forms of awakening and indeed various paths to enlightenment. Kundalini awakening normally begins with energy flowing into the body of a person, sometimes unannounced and very forcefully like it did with me. Kundalini is not a practice, nor is it a religion, a lineage, or anything that can be taught or learned. You can't "join it" or "do it"—it "does you" when it activates the Divine within. And although anything I write about Kundalini on these pages is from my own experience, generally I refer to it in the context of it being a super consciousness, a divine energetic life-force, and many other things. In terms of my own Kundalini experience, I find it hard to explain how it actually feels or affects me. This is because it's different at times, and what it's capable of doing also changes.

There seems to be an obsession with Kundalini in certain circles, and many books have been written about it. Although I have read quite a few of them, most are not worth the time because they just aren't very good. Or they've been written by people who claim to have had a Kundalini awakening but in my opinion and the opinions of others I trust, they probably did not. In reading the literature, I had to use discernment, and in so doing, I could see what was authentic and what was garbage pretty quickly. And there was a lot of garbage: Most of the books I found were about some fluffy little new age ideas of spiritual experiences, written by pseudo gurus and "teachers."

In my desperation, I have sought out many different people looking for help and guidance. As a result, I visited many of these people and/or have chatted with them through Skype. I discovered that a lot of them hadn't actually undergone a Kundalini awakening process as they'd claimed. However, I did find people who apparently had gone through a genuine Kundalini awakening. The first individual is Shellee Rae, a Reiki Master, spiritual guide, and author; she lives in Oregon. She was kind enough to share some of her experience with us here.

"Looking back in my journal, I can see symptoms of Kundalini on the move months before the big blow in April 2008. In November 2007, I was sitting in a meeting and could feel electric-like energy moving in my hands and solar plexus. It was intense heat that felt good as it coursed through me. For months after that I experienced an internal inferno combined with an emotional twister, which took the form of cyclones of energy that made me feel as if I'd spontaneously combust if I didn't find a release valve. The release usually came as tears, primal screaming, or jogging, accompanied by intense, conscious breathing. I had so much energy running through me that my whole system felt like it was on overload!

On April 9, 2008, I was entering into another meeting with some professional colleagues and was hugging people hello, as I always did. Four of these individuals, after returning my hug, said, 'Wow, what's that?' And they pointed to my heart, saying it was *very* hot. My core had been heating up all day. I had no idea that others might feel it too.

The next morning I awoke at 4:30 a.m. to a Kundalini experience. Somehow I made it to the bathroom. The fire ripping through me was too much for my body and I got sick. I had diarrhea and spat up foam and bile! The energy traveling up through my core was like a blowtorch, but even that word doesn't adequately express it. That day I felt like I'd been hit by a truck and everything seemed rather surreal. I went back to bed feeling awful, but there was something inside of me that seemed to be smiling.

A few days later I was eye-gazing (a regular practice) with a friend, which activated the energy again. Something was stirring inside of me with such beauty and wellness that I could hardly contain myself. Laughter kept bubbling out of me; the energy running through me was tickling my insides. I was up all night with heat running through my core—although it wasn't the white-hot *whoosh* that I had previously experienced. I felt like a light body and it took me a week and a half to become grounded. I also had vertigo and double vision off and on for weeks after that Kundalini activation.

Later, I had two more Kundalini experiences, one in June 2010 and another in March of 2011. The second one was much like the first had been: energy traveled from the root of my spine up to the head. The third one went from the crown down; I didn't know if I would survive that one. My brain felt like it was being broiled and when the energy hit the sacral area, that bundle of nerves lit up with pain like I've never felt before (and I've had two children!). I was paralyzed for a good twelve hours, didn't sleep for four nights, and had people coming over to take care of me for days afterward. The people who were tending me experienced "hot spots" in their bodies, frequently accompanied by a state of bliss that would last for days afterward.

What has Kundalini done for me? I noticed immediately after my first Kundalini experience that things that had previously triggered me emotionally didn't do that anymore, for instance, when I was engaging with my partner in what had previously been a difficult topic. There was nothing to defend and no one attempting to get him to 'understand.' In addition to dissolving emotional trigger, the Kundalini awakening healed emotional wounds, erased beliefs, flushed the victim, increased sensitivity, heightened intuition, deepened compassion, removed identification with various personas, and intensified the energy that comes through me while working with clients (on the energetic Reiki work I do). Last and most certainly not least, four months after the first Kundalini blast, I awakened."

The second experience of Kundalini awakening is described by Ben K. of Pennsylvania.

"Most of my adult life I was a seeker in some sense of the word. I didn't know it consciously but on some level the world just never seemed to make sense to me. Also, I had a *dis-ease* with life on an emotional level that was incredibly painful. I sought to remedy this condition with drugs, alcohol, psychology, and psychiatry. For years I fell deeper into depressive states and I was riddled with anxiety. I know now that I had been experiencing a very acute awareness of the separation from my true self, or what could be called God.

After two decades of painful decline I met a man who helped me get on a spiritual path. It started with actions taken via the 12 steps in a recovery fellowship. I had started to have the beginnings of a true spiritual awakening. The first thing that became evident to me was that my mind seemed to stop and I was able to experience the present moment without the filter of a racing and anxiety-infused mind. My mentor had me meditate and follow his directions from a Buddhist perspective.

This went well for a time but I still felt completely insane at other times and still felt darkness inside me that I feared would never leave and could end up being the death of me. Up to the point of my meeting this mentor I had no idea what spirituality was really all about. Although I had gone to church as a young child, I had never meditated and had no knowledge of Buddhism, Hinduism, or Christianity beyond what I may have heard from others.

My next experience came completely out of the blue. I was at work and I was feeling a terrible dread inside. This was normal for me but on this day it was more intense than I was used to. I can only describe the feeling as a very real sense of impending doom that created a sharp and tangible pain from my abdomen to my heart. It felt as if this pain alone could take my life. I had learned some tools from my mentor so I took a break from work and went to the bathroom to become centered and gather my thoughts. I became present with myself and felt my breath and my body. And then I said a prayer that basically was, 'God, or whatever is out there beyond myself, please relieve me of this darkness and pain.' The prayer was said from a place down in the heart of my being. I was begging to have my pain and darkness lifted.

I then went into a sort of short meditation. As I just simply followed my breath, as I had been doing now for some months in a meditation practice, I started to feel a bit of peace. Then I noticed a small, shimmering blue light. I had never seen any images or lights in my meditations leading up to this so it was puzzling to say the least. As I focused my awareness on this light it shot straight back at my awareness and sent my body back against the wall. The force was great and my head snapped back. All at once I felt euphoria and a bright light. I was still sitting with my eyes open closed and could see a bright blue-and-white light in a stream shooting up through my inner body from my pelvis out of the top of my head. Wave after wave of blissful euphoria that was too ecstatic and powerful to put into words washed through my body and spirit. It was as if I had been bathed in some sort of spiritual cleansing energy.

I sat for moments trying to recover from this experience. Once the waves settled down, I was most definitely experiencing everything through a new lens. Life would never be the same. I had no reference point for this most incredible and somewhat disturbing event.

After my initial surge of Kundalini, every time I meditated, that surge continued to gain power. At first I thought that maybe I'd had a brain aneurism. I talked to my mentor and he thought it was just some minor trick of the mind. He told me not to pay it much heed. But I knew it was something I couldn't ignore and as time went on, other phenomenon started to occur. I would meditate and the energy would come through and I would spontaneously go into yoga postures. At other times I would start to roar and even race across my floor, snarling and pawing at the air as if I were a lion. I could see spiritual truths from an experiential level that I couldn't explain. It was as if my system was being completely rewired and I was getting and still get constant downloads.

I would also understand things and know things about life that I could never have learned or read in books. As these higher and more pleasant experiences were happening, darker, scarier experiences took place too. I felt completely insane at times because painful emotions and a strong sense of disorientation would overtake me for days and weeks. At any given moment, however, I would feel quite blissful and at one with the world around me.

At one point, about six months out from my initial Kundalini experience, I heard the term *Kundalini*. I had been seeking a name for my experience and as I began to research Kundalini I knew right away that this was what was happening to me. By this time I had started to realize that this force had an intelligence and it was directing me to books and websites and even people in a very synchronistic way.

One weekend I was in a tremendous amount of spiritual pain. I felt like I had that day at work when the Kundalini first exploded through my system. I felt like I was going to die and there was another feeling inside me that I can't really explain. I did know, however, that I needed a teacher. I knew I needed someone to guide me through this Kundalini process. I said another fervent prayer and then I meditated. After this I went on the computer and typed in a phrase I had been typing in for some time with no luck. The phrase was *Kundalini support*. This yielded the local phone number of a woman who was a yoga teacher. I told her my experiences and she was shocked to say the least but also said she could help. She directed me to her guru who was just an hour away from where I lived.

The very next day I met my teacher and guru. When I met her, all of my pain and fear melted away. In the presence of this realized master I found my own Kundalini energy being soothed by some force within her. That being said, I know it's not everyone's path to have a guru or need one. It happened to be mine and for that I am so very grateful. I am still coming to terms with my life with Kundalini. Some days are dark and I wish I could be 'normal' but most days are quite amazing and I wouldn't trade my experience for anything. The biggest blessing is that I am gaining an experiential awareness of who I am beyond my mind and my body."

These are amazing accounts and I am very grateful to their authors for contributing them to this book. I have spoken to these individuals many times and have no doubt in my mind that they have had authentic Kundalini experiences. It doesn't take long to figure out when someone has indeed gone through this, for Kundalini seems to know itself when it sees itself in the world.

In my search to learn more about Kundalini, the first really good book I came across on the topic was Gopi Krishna's *The Evolutionary Energy in Man*. His Kundalini activation happened on Christmas of 1937 in Kashmir, in the north of India. The Kundalini energy rushed up his spine and into his brain in an awakening experience that was very close to mine. Gopi struggled to find someone who could frame and explain his experience and the serious ailments and torments that it manifested, including the fear that he was going insane. During his time of trial he almost died, as had I. I could certainly relate to the terror he experienced.

Gopi eventually authored a dozen books on the subject of mystical experience and the evolution of the human brain, and was internationally recognized as the foremost authority on Kundalini, the evolutionary mechanism in human beings. He travelled the world talking about it and his experience of it. Nearly every book I have read about Kundalini has quotes by or otherwise mentions Gopi Krishna. He was somewhat of a pioneer in bringing a discussion about Kundalini before the public, in the last seventy or so years anyway.

Another very good book was written by Lee Sannella, Ph.D., who wrote *The Kundalini Experience*. He made a great contribution to the treating of people with this mysterious phenomenon and those who were undergoing other mystical experiences. He also talked about psychosis and transcendence, basically explaining some of the differences between someone who was actually going mad and someone who was having a spiritual breakthrough. In an interview Sannella agreed that he had treated people who'd had spontaneous, unexpected awakenings of Kundalini, similar to my own experience. He commented that people who had these awakenings had learned not to talk about them because they might be viewed as somewhat odd, or even worse than odd—seriously afflicted.

Sannella said that there were other psychic openings but referred to Kundalini as the master opening. He agreed that in other cultures, people who have this type of awakening are encouraged and taken care of by their peers and get a very happy positive response. It's viewed as a very auspicious experience, for it's identified in a spiritual context. But here in the West there is generally no understanding of it and people need to walk this path practically alone and are viewed as psychotic or mad. At times their loved ones even abandon them.

I was very relieved to read Sanella's material and listen to his interview about Kundalini given that I had questioned my own sanity many times. Sannella said that psychosis is having no insight into all the things that are going on, and made clear that spiritual opening and psychosis can and should be distinguished, given that spiritual opening is a normal human process that man is heir to; each situation needs to be treated differently. Although sometimes it can be a fine line for some people, he also said sitting down and talking to a person in an ordinary way for a while about what was going on with them, generally would reveal what was actually taking place.

In my research I also found that Carl Jung had discussed Kundalini back in the twenties and thirties. After a trip to India, he said that we are five hundred years away from acknowledging the existence of Kundalini in the West. Even though he was a very wise man with a tremendous amount of foresight, I guess he got his timeframes wrong because I know for sure that this great life-force was awakened within me less than one hundred years after his forecast.

In any case, although nothing I could find in the literature was exactly identical to what was going on with me, the similarities and symptoms were too close for me to deny that we were talking about the same thing. And finding these similarities in the literature was very reassuring to me, to say the least.

* * *

I must have spent the next two weeks reading everything I could on the subject of Kundalini. Finding these pearls of knowledge gave me great insight, direction, and at times, motivation on my personal path, given the overwhelming challenges I was facing. For it was indeed proving to be difficult to find my way in a society that wasn't very aware of/barely recognized the precise thing that had become the single most important thing in my life.

It was comforting, however, to know that I wasn't in the grips of a wicked illness—although some religious fundamentalists out there would have me believe that I was, or that I had tapped into some satanic force—which is absolute nonsense. As I write this, there are people dwelling in ashrams in the East who are under the direction of a guru who is trying to activate their Kundalini. That's definitely a safer way to go, as the person can prepare and cleanse the system for such an experience. But I even question that practice today, for I wonder how prepared one can really be for what may be the traumatic experience of a Kundalini awakening. Indeed, the actual experience might not be what you had in mind and once it activates into the human system, it's game over—there is no putting that particular gene back in the bottle, like I said already, those who set out to awaken it very rarely do.

In short, I don't recommend that anyone should forcefully try to bring the Kundalini up. I certainly wasn't prepared for my Kundalini experience, which is what's called "a spontaneous awakening." It sent me straight into a syndrome-type of situation with no guru or teacher to guide me out of it. Furthermore, it took me nearly two years to find out what had actually happened. I had to become my own guru and find my own help. My house was on fire big time, to the point where it nearly killed me.

* * *

Kundalini has as many different faces as humanity itself, and presents in a myriad of ways. And although the word *Kundalini* has become a little more common in our society today, most people really don't know what it actually is or what it really means. Nor does Western medicine recognize it, although what I find remarkable, as mentioned earlier in this book, is that the caduceus—the image of the uncoiled serpent that we see in medical settings—is Kundalini's symbol.

It used to be thought that only holy people or practiced yogis experienced Kundalini, but that's totally changed. However, just because one has energy buzzing around their system, doesn't necessarily mean one is undergoing a Kundalini awakening. I myself have met a nice number of people that actually do have it, all of them just regular everyday folks. Some of these people have become my friends. I even met a lady from Ireland who was going through it; and she was a great help to me when I was struggling with my own process of transformation.

Every person with activated Kundalini who I have spoken with has a different story to tell, invariably replete with various manifestations of visions, paranormal activities, astral travel, dark entities, cleansing patterns, and physical ailments. The list goes on and on. However, the structure of the awakening always seems to be the same: It takes the form of the inner energetic upheaval articulated earlier. Although most people experience Kundalini racing up the spine, I have found other people who have had Kundalini awakenings through their heart. My first Kundalini awakening back in 2007 came through my heart, although this type of awakening appears to be less common. (I will elaborate on this heart-opening form of Kundalini a little later in this chapter.)

In general, the awakening process can go on for many years, as it did with me, or it may continue until the death of the physical body. As the process continues, all of the material that the Kundalini sets off becomes active in the body's subtle energy fields, which are basically everything that's invisible in our aura. This includes thoughts, emotions, consciousness, and the different sensors of the body—the main ones being the body's seven chakras.

As we have established, the unfolding of this process can be a very painful experience filled with fear. As the awakening is created and the consciousness is expanded, the person begins to view life from a very different place than they did before. In my own experience the shift in my consciousness was so extreme that I became ungrounded and couldn't function. Another symptom was that of body heat or lack thereof: At times heat would flood through my body and then in the next moment I would be freezing.

It's important to understand that it's not the actual energy that stresses out the system, it's the blockages that it runs into during the cleansing process. In me, along with other manifesting symptoms, this caused a chronic hormonal imbalance that created problems with my thyroid gland, which is the butterfly-shaped gland in the throat that influences one's metabolism, among many other bodily functions. Over a period of time I experienced a weight gain of almost thirty pounds. This might not sound like a lot, but it was remarkable in that I was exercising and very carefully monitoring my diet and caloric input at that time.

I visited my doctor to explain this dilemma to him. He tried to tell me I was over forty years old and it was common to put on weight at my age, but I refused to leave it at that and had tests done. Of course, as I expected, the test results didn't show anything wrong with me, given that it's difficult to trace Kundalini symptomatology with Western medicine and present-day medical technology. It certainly won't show up on an X-ray machine. That being the case, I *have* found some people in the medical field who have written about Kundalini and have made substantial contributions in trying to educate people on the subject. In my own case, I asked my doctor if he had heard of Kundalini energy. At first he ignored me, then he asked me in an uninterested way what it was. I didn't even reply. Most doctors I have met are ego maniacs who cant treat people beyond where their education has brought them. They care more about what the lab results state instead of actually listening to and treating the patient..

It's a shame really, that in indigenous cultures when someone had such an experience and had been blessed with awakened Kundalini, "shaman's sickness," a near-death experience, or the many different mystical experiences that can happen—they became honored by the rest of their people and invariably went on to become a revered medicine man, shaman, or healer within their village. How much things have changed in today's Western world. Spirituality was really important to the people who preceded us as they didn't have the material luxuries we have today. We have the material progress but the spiritual part doesn't seem to be as important to our generation. I wonder if this is why so many humans are depressed miserable zombies and stuck on pharmaceutical drugs. I bet the indigenous people weren't on antidepressants. Nor did they need 12-step programs. I wonder who the happiest, most fulfilled, and more contented people were?

Today it's more important for people to be involved with, and obsess over the comical politicians we watch on our TV screens—who don't care about anything but themselves and their wealth, greed, and power. Something has to change. I believe it's slowly happening and that more and more people are awakening and are turning to the world of spirit as they do so.

In any event, in my own case when my doctor clearly was not interested in my experience of Kundalini awakening, I focused my energy on doing a lot of detective work on my own by speaking with others who'd undergone a similar experience and who had some of the same problems I did. Most of my help came from and continues to come from fellow healers and from what I can research on my own. There are some good healthcare professionals out there who work with traditional medicines and can help someone in a Kundalini awakening process. Although they may understand your plight they tend to be few and far between and difficult to find. I found an amazing nutritionist at my local health food store who knew about Kundalini awakening and guided me to supplements that helped to heal my nervous system as well as my immune system.

In addition to the weight gain, I had been experiencing chronic fatigue and a low sex drive for a few years, and these things weren't getting better by themselves. This taught me that I couldn't rely on the Kundalini energy to cleanse, fix, and heal *everything* that was wrong with me even with it being Divine energy. I would have to play my part, which often proved to be difficult. However, between the collapse of my ego and the physical ailments I was experiencing, I learned a lot of lessons. Things that I used to do for pleasure or to fulfill a warped idea of fun didn't seem appealing anymore.

This was strange at the outset, for I was no longer being driven to be materially successful or have any type of power over my fellow human being. None of that really mattered anymore, even though I struggled with fears of survival for a time. All of this probably sounds strange to anyone trying to make their mark in the material realm; I guess a life devoid of ambition doesn't make sense to most people. One of the great gifts that the Kundalini has brought me is that I don't worry about the future too much, or the past anymore, for a lot of the old data and the memory patterns surrounding the data have been erased.

Another gift, even though I didn't view it as a gift at the beginning because I couldn't really understand what it was all about, was the fact that I could see spiritual truths about people that apparently no one else could see. At times my ego would dissolve and I could look right at people and see everything that was true and false about them. Be that as it may, I had to learn to honor and meet people where they were. I also had to stop being a people pleaser, which is a trait that I can no longer get away with. I must be true to myself or it causes me problems. As such, Kundalini is an intelligent internal mechanism that keeps driving me back to be grounded in integrity. And the more I have become in touch with this, the less I get away with. In this way I have a very sensitive but more profound connection to other people and to energy in general.

I am operating from a totally different place than what I used to, a much higher frequency, and I have access to things that I never had access to before. Specifically, I have a much broader understanding of my life, the person I used to be, and the changes that have taken place. The weird thing but also the exciting thing with Kundalini is that I don't know what will happen from one day to the next. It's a total adventure, as well as a super challenge. Each morning I wake up determined to stay open to the possibilities of what might transpire that day.

* * *

As time went on, I began to wonder how my Kundalini had been activated. Was it the accident on the power plant when the base of my spine had cracked? Or was it as result of my years of meditation and all the different spiritual practices I had engaged in during my recovery from drugs and alcohol? I still don't have the definitive answer to this but I believe that it may have introduced itself to me back in 2007 when I thought I was losing my mind. I recall my sister coming over from Ireland to take care of me given that I wasn't doing very well, but I couldn't explain to her what was wrong with me as I didn't understand it myself.

It was around this time, in 2007, that I had gone through a divorce, although attributing my Kundalini experience to my divorce doesn't really make sense given that I hadn't wanted to be in the marriage for quite some time. The divorce had been, in many ways, a relief. In any event, when I initially had the Kundalini experience, it came through my heart. The energy center in my heart chakra felt like it had burst open. The result was that I felt extreme bouts of compassion for other people and their oftentimes dire situations. I couldn't stop crying and didn't know why, although looking back on it, all the crying might have been a way of cleansing and detoxing. I now posit that this may have been the first manifestation of my "spiritual opening." Starting with my heart, the Kundalini did whatever work it needed to do. Then it simmered right down until almost four years later, in late 2010, when my construction accident occurred. At this time, it awakened at the base of my spine and rose upward in what's known as "the spinal sweep."

Some folks say you travel many lifetimes to have Kundalini activated. I have no proof of that, neither do I know if I was born with it. I do know one thing; it's been a very strange life for the most part and I was undergoing some crazy shit after my accident. I was still very ungrounded and my energy field was wide open and unfiltered. Although the work with Penney and Janice had helped tremendously with that, I still had a long way to go.

I would read how the Kundalini energy intelligently rewires the cells in the body and brain, with the person receiving the potential for great wisdom and intellect and many other special powers the Kundalini sometimes gives the person access to prior to the bestowal of enlightenment. I couldn't help but be amazed that I was experiencing this mysterious energy and having this mystical experience that had been sought out by certain serious spiritual seekers through the ages, and hidden within ancient scriptures. When it arrived uninvited within me, I was stunned, to be honest.

Of course the ego grabbed a hold of it and triggered its daft stories about how I was now very special. This is a very dangerous place to go and one has to be careful who one talks to in spiritual circles about this type of thing. This is because if they've had a similar experience they may believe that they are very special as well. I needed to get away from that as quickly as possible and keep my feet planted on planet earth.

Ego inflation has been one of the most difficult parts of my whole journey for it is capable of causing major blockages and problems. Indeed, some people even say that the Kundalini does most of its work at night while the person sleeps because the ego is out of the way then. My ego had been continuously getting in the way with its stories of wanting and needing enlightenment, and other madness. I soon worked through all that by talking about it to my recovery network, which helped erase those stories. Ego inflation is so subtle and can do serious damage by disconnecting one from the rest of mankind. This is a sure sign that a person is in trouble and missing the boat big time. Sometimes a skillful teacher or guru may be required to help a person through this difficult phase, given that the self-deception can be very thick. True awakening will always bring one closer to being of greater service to humanity with a connected sense of oneness.

Things started to make more sense to me when I got over the initial shock of what was occurring. The opening and cleansing of the chakras was like air vents opening and closing, letting the old toxic material out and the fresh air in. Thus it was with the energies entering and exiting my body. This process was made more challenging by the fact that I was living in New York with so much happening energetically.

As mentioned earlier, my experience made me much more sensitive and in tune with the energies of others. That said, it made sense why I often didn't feel very comfortable in recovery meetings anymore. I could feel things in such a deep way, in a way where there was no separation between myself and other people's energy fields. This made it particularly difficult to be around any type of dark energy. I don't mean I was judging people on their bad points or critiquing them on their defects. I was taking their energy on, like a custom-made suit, and wearing it, which would exhaust and choke me at times. I was like a magnet for a myriad of dark emotions—anger, fear, dishonesty, manipulation, and jealousy. Whatever was coming my way, I would take on and in so doing, I would feel the exact same emotions that the people around me were feeling. This was because my body and all of its cells were awakening too.

I couldn't even read the newspaper, for if it contained a negative story about a rape or the harm done to a child I would automatically take on that vibe. I would invariably be very sad and effected by it, to the point of not wanting to live in this world anymore, trying to explain this to people got me very weird looks so I soon stopped that. Subways and shopping malls were also no-go areas, as were any places that a lot of people congregated. As a result of this energetic overload, I spent a lot of time at home alone or alone in nature, which was a great comfort to me.

I think everyone has the capacity to have this same level of sensitivity for it's imprinted in our DNA. The difference is, most people stay asleep and clogged up like dirty slop sinks. The Kundalini had dislodged and freed up a lot of old stuff and I had relived a lot of karma with the obsessive cleanses that had been coming through my system for a few years at this point. The Kundalini melted through my stuff, releasing it into my body from the depths of my soul, then rolled it all through my mind. As it did so, it worked on removing different obsessions, like the one for booze. It erased the victim mentality from me also along with all other types of fears, habits and thought processes. Even though my whole life has been changed irrevocably forever, my Kundalini awakening process continues on. As it does, I continue to adapt to the outside world so that I can peacefully co-exist with the rest of the planet.

*

All sorts of paranormal activities were happening, even before I knew it was Kundalini I had. I went through a long period were I would see people's souls when I looked at them. This is different than taking on their energy as I've described above. A typical soul that I saw would appear to have a fleshy mound around it, which was the body. I generally saw this in strangers as I walked down the street.

I walked down Sixth Avenue in Manhattan on my lunch break one day and that's all I could see around me: people's souls. It was the strangest thing ever. I spoke to my friend on the phone and asked him what he saw when he looked at people. When he'd stopped speaking, I told him what I'd been seeing, and he replied, "Wow! I'm definitely not seeing *that!*"

At the beginning, seeing all these souls was intense and very disorientating. Thank God that's leveled off. I have to really pay attention today if I want to look deeply into what's going on with someone. I also have to be invited. I wouldn't peek through a window at a women getting undressed as it's creepy.

A variety of other activities would occur, not all the time, but often enough. When I was back in Belfast in 2013 I had the strongest urge to place bets on a few horses. For two days in a row, I collected on two big outside shots with nice odds. I tried it again the next day only with no urge this time and I didn't win.

I awoke one morning and remembered there was a football final on that day. As I did so, a score registered briefly on the surface of my mind, long enough for me to remember it and notice it in an authentic way. I went back to check the score from the match when it was over. It was exactly the same score that had come to me that morning. I would also receive different precognitions about what might happen in the future. For example, I thought about two people from my recovery group and saw that they were going to start dating, and a couple of days later they did. I had a dream I was going to get laid off from my job. I thus began to pay close attention to the energy at work and could clearly see it was coming, even when my boss lied to me and told me it wasn't. Then, right out nowhere, it sure enough occurred a few days later. I wasn't saying *maybe* this stuff was going happen. I *knew* it was going to happen, and the strange thing was I just got on with my life without even being bothered by it. The truth is, we're all far more connected than many of us like to believe we are.

Here's another example: I was walking through the job site one day when I started to think about a guy I hadn't seen in thirteen years. Nor had I even thought much about him for that matter. I turned the corner and there he was, standing right in front of me. I couldn't make this stuff happen; it would occur and roll through my energy field. To be honest, I wasn't startled or even surprised, for it actually felt quite natural. In any event, I never shared what was happening with anyone; I just kept it to myself.

I read about people with Kundalini having access to certain powers (*siddhis* as they are known in Sanskrit) that weren't extant before activation. I found this very interesting. My ego remained very uninvolved and was quiet about all the new activity. I think it was stunned and totally collapsed and couldn't comment. It probably had a problem with the whole idea of being up against the Kundalini. It was on its hind legs and on the way out and it probably knew its time was almost up and thus it wouldn't have the power it used to have over me.

Chapter 10
The Kundalini Ring Brings Everything Full Circle

The Kundalini brought everything about me to the surface—every aspect of my personality that was negative or the things from my past that still hadn't been resolved. It was all put under a life-size magnifying glass and amplified. Some of my deepest darkest fears haunted me constantly. Memories of bad things I had done to people when I was younger would appear and I would view them and feel them with such shame and sorrow that it would make me want to cry at times. The strange thing with Kundalini is that these thoughts and fears would seem ten times worse than usual—very overpowering. This was especially true if several memories collided all at once, which added to the stress of what was occurring in my current life circumstances. The dishonesty that I had brought into relationships I had been in . . . the bitterness I had caused other people . . . I didn't seem to be getting away with anything.

Subsequent to reliving the bad memories, the ego chatter would start. It would reveal how much of a loser I was for my bad behavior and otherwise rip me to shreds. That's when I learned that I had to cut myself some slack and try to forgive myself. It was very difficult to survive in modern Western society with all of this transpiring. When these cleansings were happening the last place I could be was around a negative person so a lot of people had to be cut out of my life as I learned how to process and release all the energies in me that needed clearing.

Meditation was vital when moving through these times as were long walks by myself, given that the karma would burn off in cycles of past memories. I began to notice that the childhood and sometimes adult memories that would come through my mind's eye would sometimes recycle and travel back through without feeling the emotion that had once accompanied the memory. For the most part, most of the thoughts and emotions would eventually just fall away, leaving me in a state of presence. It seemed like the death of the self. Prior to my "awakening" I'd had many different interests that I was passionate about. However, somehow in this cleansing process the interests were demolished.

As the Kundalini dug up the sludge and poison from the depths of my soul, I had to start using discernment about which people I could be around, what type of food I could eat, and the people and places that needed to be sidestepped. I just wanted it all to stop, but when it didn't seem to be, I became desperate to find more answers. One thing I did know: the Kundalini energy would get stuck if it hit unresolved emotional issues in the body and at times it would stick in me big time. I couldn't always tell what emotional issues would leave the energy stuck although sometimes I could also feel what part of the body it was stuck in. It would become stagnant and stick in the lower Chakras causing extreme back pain and other pains around my pelvis and stomach.

When I read that yoga could help get the energy flowing, I found myself in a variety of yoga studios. Some people in those circles were very helpful and I met a couple of yoga teachers who tried to help me out but generally no one knew what Kundalini really was, and I was very cautious who I asked. I found a lot of people who were quick to claim they had insight into these questions, and their practices would help me, but I wasn't feeling it most of the time. There are so many posers and pretenders out there in designer yoga pants these days and most of these folks didn't seem interested in growing spiritually. Instead, it was all about the image, with the OM tattoo on the wrist and a hot body.

The negative energies of people around me would have one effect on me, but I also found the opposite to be true. People who really cared about me, or a positive thing that was said to me, or a quick phone call to my mentor or friends could change my whole day. These were the things I found that grounded me and brought me back down out of the clouds. These were the things that brought me peace and contentment. Even if it was only for ten minutes it would be a small victory—and all those small victories added up and meant something. Watching soccer games and reading articles in the newspaper about my team would be grounding, as would hearing my daughter's voice on the other end of the phone. It would bring me to earth for a while and get me out of my head, as would looking at pictures of my family and other things that had a place in my heart. Sometimes I would just lie on my bed, listening to soft happy music and praying.

Kundalini is the real teacher. It was calling the shots, it had an agenda, and I needed to find whatever it took to get with that program. Over and over again, it let me know what needed to change in my life. If I didn't listen, my body would be in pain. For instance, at times I got violently sick after eating a certain food that my body really wanted nothing to do with, and I had to remove it from my diet. I have learned this bitter lesson quite a few times. The same holds true about my surroundings, people I hang out with, what I view on TV or indeed anything that my energy field comes in contact with—it strives for purity of my vision also.

There's a saying in recovery circles that I used to find comfort in, "God will never give you any more than you can handle." I just smile to myself when I hear those words today and think *OMG, that just isn't my truth anymore.* I know for sure that God will totally give me more than I can handle, for the simple reason that so doing brings me closer and closer to the divine nature. Having it my way all the time won't do that; living the high life never brought me closer to my higher self. I thank God I am still walking on my own two feet and sober, and for the people He has put in my path to assist my healing inside and outside of recovery. I have been blessed in so many ways.

* * *

The year was 2013 and life went on, and even with the newfound information I had, I continued to try to work for the next few years. I was running around the place, half awake and suffering, and my life was one big struggle from one day to the next. I had a problem dealing with dishonest company owners and coworkers—some people are just scumbags. Indeed, anything or anyone who was being unauthentic would cause me turmoil and it seemed like most people were in the big hustle to get ahead.

I was sitting in the shanty one morning getting ready for the day. All the big company bosses were there having a meeting and I could see their fear and greed and how they wanted to motivate the work force with fear. I could see the whole show for what it was and I just wanted to laugh out loud in all their faces, but thank God I was grounded enough to know not to do that. I wasn't buying it anymore; not fully anyway. I had been pushed to a whole new level of consciousness and a radically different way of living, and as a result, my work surroundings generally sickened me.

At times I wished for the old ignorant dream state as I trudged through this new purgatory. Or a desire to go live by the ocean or in the mountains would come over me. But then I would realize the impossibility of giving up my day job, given how sorely I needed the money, or thought I did. (I have since learned that was my ego talking.) Sometimes I ran a whole crew of ironworkers with as many as fifteen-plus guys in it, my eyes and ears had to be open all day as I was in charge of heavy steel and panels being lifted high above the streets of New York City. If anything should go wrong, people could die. My job was exhausting and I was under a tremendous amount of pressure each and every day which would stress my system out to no end. The fatigue would cripple me and hinder my movements to no end as I ran up and down flights of stairs and climbing on steel all day trying to keep things moving along.

If a problem arose I would have to think quickly to solve it. At times my head was in a haze with brain fog that brought short term memory loss and I couldn't think straight. Other times my neck would be snapping into kriyas. Even though it sounds like any other job, I found it utterly overwhelming. I was dealing with greedy higher-ups who were never satisfied as they sat back collecting the dough while everyone else took the pressure. I wouldn't buy their bullshit and found myself unable to condone their fear-based motivational tactics. So I would stand my ground until I couldn't, at which point there would be a shouting match and eventually I would just quit as I didn't want to deal with them anymore. I would leave that environment and take a few weeks off and then go back and begin the same process all over again.

What became very obvious to me early on was that I had to forgive people that I got into scrapes with and apologize quickly or I would be handicapped by guilt and resentment on levels that I had never known. Extreme guilt would bring me right down and the Kundalini energy made it feel ten times worse.

Carrying on trying to make a living brought me all over New York to jobs and situations that I had once enjoyed; the union always kept me busy. I did everything from dragging heavy iron across decks in the blistering sun in the Bronx all day, off-loading trucks of heavy steel, to welding heavy-duty iron in ninety-plus degree heat on Manhattan high-rises in the middle of summer. Or I'd be off-loading trucks of steel into the dark of night in the winter *and* summer. The strain and pain on my body was intense and sometimes I only kept going because I was working with a good bunch of guys. My nervous system always seemed on high alert and I'd live in hope that I would get it all together and find a comfortable place to operate from again.

Every morning the alarm clock would go off at 4:30 a.m. and every morning it seemed like I had never slept. I would get out of bed and then would sit on my chair and try to get focused. Next I would mediate, pray, and get ready to make it through another day. I'd put on my boots and walk to the train in some of the strangest most horrible states a person could imagine. Here I was, this guy waking up in the middle of one of the craziest cities in the world. I had Kundalini and felt like I was stuck between different realms. I dreaded each day, as I was going to do work that I had come to hate, but I continued on as I couldn't see any other way. I would take the number seven train to work, into a career that my body and soul were screaming to me that I should get away from.

As I said earlier, I wasn't ready to pay attention. Money seemed to be a serious attachment and was blocking me from living a simpler life. Fear would grip me about not being able to pay the bills—and what would I do about retirement? Or how about insurance if I got sick? That fucking ego! Don't believe anyone who tells you the path of Kundalini awakening is an easy one. I'm skeptical of anyone who claims they had no difficulty—believe me, I have found nothing tougher.

* * *

Living two stops on the train from Jackson Heights in Queens made for a very interesting experience each morning as I walked to the train and got on it. This area is one of the most ethnically diverse locations on the planet, with dozens of different languages being spoken.

There were typically a wide assortment of somber gloomy energies on the train each morning and these toxic energies would make me sick. Subway cars and stations are some of the most difficult places I had to pace through, for they had some of the dirtiest sleazy energies I have ever felt and been around . . . the stench of urine from the bum lying on the seat beside me to the anxious energy I would pick up from the homeless veteran panhandling for money so he could eat breakfast . . . I felt so raw and open without a filter. Some mornings I would step back off the train and return home as I couldn't deal with it all—it would make me so tired and confused I would lie down on my bed for five or six hours as continuing on that day seemed impossible.

On the days that I did power through, however, en route to work I would reach Manhattan, climb the steep steps up onto Lexington Avenue or whatever station I was working beside. My legs would be in agony, feeling like they were rubber and had a mind of their own; my muscles had been frazzled by the Kundalini energy doing its work, and by the unresolved blockages that it was hitting. I would hit the street in the freezing cold of winter or the hot sweating humid mornings of summer. It didn't matter as both seasons caused me problems, although the stations didn't stink as much and the energy didn't seem to be as grimy when it was cold. Puffing and panting up the steps onto the street I would be unsure what to eat for breakfast, for our society is riddled with delis that carry unhealthy foods loaded with starches, sugars, and GMOs—none of which are good for a person in the midst of a Kundalini awakening. This was another very difficult lesson for me to learn. I couldn't find any kind of discipline and consistency in terms of my food's preparation even though New York is one of the best cities of the world in which to find healthy food.

When it was clear that a major change in my diet had to take place, I went on an almost totally organic diet that was pure and GMO-free (although I have my cheat moments still). The body truly is a temple, and that becomes an intense reality for a Kundalini person, as Kundalini is divine energy—the only thing it cares about is achieving purity and it will be very forceful to get to that place if it has to. I was in a part of the process where I should have been resting and eating as much organic produce as I could get my hands on, not welding and breathing in unhealthy fumes from 7018 welding rods that were hotter than the sun, with smog coming off them that made me choke and cough all day.

I learned that a sugar-free, caffeine-free diet, with as much raw organic produce as possible was best for my system, given my condition, with sometimes a little meat for grounding purposes. Be this as it may, my ego would do battle to have its way. Eating the proper food would bring about an inspirational, fluent type of vibration at times, as if the energy was delighted. However, eating something that wasn't good for me would land me on the toilet right away, with all kinds of pains and strange sensations in my body, accompanied by killer headaches. This was akin to eating something that I was allergic to and getting a really bad reaction. I very quickly learned that fast food was a no-go, although I had never been keen on it from the start. My body now felt sickened by and rejected other stuff I had eaten and enjoyed all my life. It took me time to discover what my newly arranged body could handle and what it couldn't; it was sensitive to some of the favorite things I had eaten since I was boy. That's a strange experience: discovering that some of my favorite foods now repulsed me.

Coffee would buzz out my whole nervous system and make me feel like I was a rocket ship ready to take off. I drank coffee for the first five years of my Kundalini awakening, quitting for ten months and five months in that time, and I could feel the difference. However, I always went back to it, and eventually it almost burnt out my system as a result of overworking it. I don't recommend that anyone with Kundalini drink a lot of coffee.

I actually went through a period when I had no desire to do anything in this life. I was in a very dark spiritual depression (otherwise known as "the dark night of the soul" in spiritual circles), during which time nothing could fulfill me.

One of my teachers calls this "the rich place." My desire to go on dates and meet a girl was nonexistent, which was odd because this had been one of my favorite things to do in the past. However, now it became really difficult to meet anyone who piqued my interest. I went through a time when the small talk and the other things you do on a date just didn't seem interesting anymore; it seemed superficial. A lot of this would change when I became more grounded and more accustomed to the new way I was experiencing life. I understood that if I was to continue to live in this culture, then I must find a way to do that.

It's plain to see for me today why people might take their own life or find themselves in a psyche ward type of situation. It comes from not obeying what this super powerful intelligent energy is trying to convey to you. That might be difficult if the person can't figure out what is wrong with them. The shift that takes place practically within seconds creates such a gap as to what life once looked like and what it looks like now, just like in my own situation. After a while you must pay attention to the signs the body is giving you. The body never lies. Instead, if you listen, it lets you know what to do and what not to do. However, that said, you may still need some guidance from a trustworthy teacher until you find your own feet and can follow the signs by yourself. There are some great books out there that will help, but use prudence and don't ever do anything that seems unethical or immoral to your beliefs—no matter what the teacher tells you, be that a book or a person. If it feels off, then it *is* off, and it's not for you.

My life had changed so much and was continuing to do so. I had done weight training for a lot of my life—kickboxing, running, and always some type of sport to keep fit—but I had not been able to do any of that anymore. I was continuously trying to get in a good workout at the gym, and every once in a while I would succeed, but then I would suffer for days, aching and exhausted. It became obvious that I had to stop doing those activities, for the time being, anyway.

Clearly my energy needed to be preserved for the Kundalini to carry out its work. I tried different forms of yoga also, but I had picked up so many injuries at work that I was totally limited in terms of the activities I could do. It was, however, important for me to get whatever exercise I could when my body would permit me to do so, and generally that was just a walk. This would help the flow, as lying around doing nothing would cause static and that would create problems.

* * *

One day I was over on the West Side of Manhattan near Tenth Avenue. I then entered a deli to get a drink. I heard a voice say "OMG! Adrian Clarke—I haven't seen you in years!" It was an old friend of the family who I hadn't seen for seventeen years. We chatted for a while with the usual protocol of small talk that comes with someone you haven't seen in a long time. When we said our good-byes and I was walking away, she remembered about a box of items belonging to my brother and asked if I would like them. She told me that it contained photos of the family and there was also a ring inside the box. I got the impression she didn't want to hold onto it any longer, so I agreed to take it.

It was a couple of weeks later when I ventured back over to the West Side to pick up the box. I recall sitting in the back of a cab that night, riding across the city, looking through the contents of the box. I looked through the pictures of my family. Some of them I hadn't seen in many years, others I had never seen before. They were digging up old memories, for they were of times gone by: my sisters' weddings, and family vacations abroad.

My dad's old seaman union book was in there also. Wrapped in a handkerchief I could feel something solid underneath. I unwrapped it and found a gold ring inside. It was a gold serpent with a single ruby for the eye. I had remembered that ring as a child. It was my father's. He had bought it in Belfast and then passed it along to my brother. I had totally forgotten about it and found it very strange that it had surfaced now. It was cracked in the back and very dirty. Somehow it had found its way into this box, which had survived a serious house fire that had nearly ruined everything else. It had remained intact and I could tell it hadn't been out of the box for many years.

My brother asked me for the photos and told me I could keep the ring. I never would have asked for it as I'm not the type to wear jewelry. The significance of it hadn't dawned on me yet. I left it with a jeweler to be fixed, sized, and polished, and it came back to me immaculate. The figure on the ring was that of a serpent coiled three and half times; the unmistakable symbol of the mysterious Kundalini. It blew my mind when I realized how this was another one of those wonderful synchronicities that my path of Kundalini awakening has been laced with.

Chapter 11
Holding Fast While the Karma Continues to Clear

I'll never forget the day I left Belfast to start a new life in New York City. It was February 2002. I had been impressed with NYC ever since my trip to visit my brother Mark in 1990, and then again when I'd tried to make a go of living there in 1997. I was exactly three hundred and sixty-six days sober, twenty-seven years old, and afraid for my life. It was difficult to leave the new spiritual community I had become such a part of for it had undoubtedly saved my skin and set me on a different path.

Life was strange enough in early recovery without moving to the other side of the globe, wondering what was waiting for me, and having to start all over again. But even worse than that, I had to leave my family and the country of my birth. Something broke inside me when I left. You can forget things, find and learn new things, and meet new people. But underneath it all, it's never the same when you leave your own people and land.

Looking back over the bigger decisions I had to make, I can now see that I was forced by life to make them. This was certainly another of those decisions. I had met a girl a few years previously. We had kept in touch and kept running into each other between my visits to New York and her visits to Ireland. She had gotten pregnant so I had a major life-changing decision to make. I made up my mind to give it another try in the States. I couldn't fathom what it would be like to have a daughter, never seeing her and always be wondering about her.

This was enough to prompt me to move.

All my friends, the things I was raised on, the streets that I knew so well, and the people that lived on them who had been my lifelong friends—I was fretting over leaving them all. I would leave my heritage and a culture that I really loved. I'm proud to be Irish—but everything was going to change. My regular trips to Scotland on the ferry with all my friends to see my beloved

Celtic play would be gone. That had been such a part of who I was, it was hard to imagine my life without it. All I had to take across the world with me were a few belongings and memories in my mind.

So, with an aching heart and two big bags with all my stuff in them, I got into my uncle Tony's taxi. I couldn't really bear to look back because my family was standing at the front door of my parents' house to see me off—my grandmother, nephews, nieces, sisters, friends and everyone. My father wasn't there. He had called to let me know he wouldn't be home on time, but I knew he was just like me and couldn't really stomach the whole good- bye thing. His way of handling that was easier for both of us. Besides, my dad loved his trips to New York so I knew I would see him again soon.

I thought I was embarking on a journey to make the American dream come true, and in a lot of ways I was. However, I would only find that the happiness and security it promised would not be long lasting. It was not long lasting because none of it was permanent. That didn't stop me from getting sucked up into the New York hustle for many years, however.

My experience was to be more like the American nightmare a lot of the time, when I was asleep to myself and life—eventually everything I tried to fulfill myself with ceased to satisfy. Don't get me wrong, I enjoyed so much of it, met some wonderful people, made some amazing friends, landed an excellent job, made some real money, and even became a citizen with a U.S. passport who got to vote in elections. I can now see that there was no better place this whole experience could have unfurled than New York City. At the back of everything I thought I was coming here for something else. What I couldn't see is that it was a different type of voyage I was on—a journey of healing, a pilgrimage into the soul that would lead me home. That venture really doesn't have anything to do with prizes and possessions. Years of suffering landed me on this path—and I don't like suffering!

Western society is set up by its leaders to have us believe that happiness and joy lay out in the material realm. They don't ever want us to know that true happiness, joy, and peace is something that is found within. Or perhaps they just don't know that themselves. I strongly doubt that many of them do. If the majority of people in the West discovered that truth and found ways to help each other experience true happiness, can you imagine the effect it would have on this world? It would tear down the huge pharmaceutical industry and put an end to the wars that are really only started for financial and powerful gain. If we believe the advertising that's on the screens and billboards or everywhere else we look these days, then the impression given is that we can only *buy* happiness.

The sad truth is that we have all been programmed to believe that happiness can only be found in the next new thing we purchase or when our next desire is fulfilled. We are programmed to believe that we live in the land of the free, when really we've been tricked into living in the prison between our ears. What is the next addition I can make to my life to solve this inner conundrum of unrest and turmoil? I'm convinced I will find lasting satisfaction in something "out there."

I chased after this illusion for most of my life, eventually realizing that it's a damp firework that never goes off. Although wealth can definitely make life more comfortable, lasting happiness and peace can never be found in the next new thing. This is a fact of my experience!

I have watched people land in psych wards or take their own lives pursuing this dream. Sometimes they got everything they wanted and more and other times they didn't, but the end result looked the same: "unhappy and discontented." Some of these people I knew personally had enough wealth to last them several lifetimes, but it still didn't solve their dilemma. For many years I was hypnotized like most other people, trying to accumulate "more" and failing miserably in the end. And the more I failed in obtaining these resources, the more suffering came into my life. This led to me being interested and curious about the spiritual path.

Even my interaction with females for most of my life was all about finding happiness and peace in the next girl, only to move along to the next, to soon find I was bored or unfulfilled yet again. I was unconscious of this pattern for most of my life as I jumped from one girl to the next—some of them wonderful human beings. At some point, I became conscious of the fact that I was the one with the problem and it had to be solved within me. Partner jumping is a red flag that something's not right, as is excessive spending, eating, gambling—we could add several more pages to this list.

These were all just ways I had found to cope with the underlying anxiety I had been harboring for nearly all of my life. I wasn't really even aware of this anxiety most of the time as I became so used to living with it and suppressing it by distracting myself from it, with whatever the mind pointed at next. But it would cause dysfunction, and that would send me on a wild goose chase looking for more things to fix the dysfunction with, or at least ways to cover it up so it appeared that I fit in with everyone else. Through all this I would tell myself I was happy, but aren't you supposed to be? When you have risen to that rung that society calls successful, the more things you have, the more successful you are. Right?

* * *

In the end everything played its part and eventually the universe pushed and prodded me until I was forced to look in the place that I had been afraid of. This was the place that I had run away from through alcoholism and many other things—right inside. I was under some sort of belief that I had been thorough in my recovery program. And indeed, the 12 steps had taken me deep, but as my experience unfurled I came to see that I had only scratched the surface. However, I did open a door into my soul all the same. I have no doubt that my recovery work saved my life and made for better living. That's why I really love and respect the recovery community so much, although I wish a lot of people in that community would be more courageous and dig deeper on their spiritual quest. But it does save so many lives; it's still a great joy to watch that happen.

My perseverance and devotion to that process of recovery had blown the doors wide open and given me such an appetite to go seek in the world's different theologies and goody bags of spirituality. I knew there was so much more, and I'm glad I didn't listen to some of the cranky and miserable underdeveloped elders who tried to deter me from going any further. They would tell me things like, "Don't be looking for something that's not there," or "Don't try to get something out of life that's not possible," "Don't wait for the other shoe to drop, kid," just because they were afraid and too undisciplined to continue searching themselves. Or, in a lot of cases, they were delusional that they were on some great search. Never let anyone hold you back! Leave them behind and keep walking.

Some of the new spiritual practices and books I found were great, some were good, and some were garbage. Remember, again, a lot of so-called healers, teachers, and/or gurus are just out to make some bucks, promising a speedy way to enlightenment. That's a red flag; there is no weekend workshop on that, or any five-step process. These promises of quick fixes and easy steps to a better life don't actually exist. Enlightenment comes to very few. I was to find my endeavor with spiritual seeking interesting and exciting.

I was having such a different experience with this, compared to how I had felt about religion growing up, which I hadn't accepted. I was finding this material more tailored for me. It was like crossing the river in a boat. When you reached the other side you got out and kept going, leaving that boat behind. New river new boat—exact same concept I found with the different spiritual material that I would later seek out. I would work with a new meditation practice for several weeks or months to see if it was any good and if not, I would dump it and try something new. I did this until I found something that did work and helped make my life better.

I had the freedom to approach whatever I wanted whenever I wanted. I didn't need to commit to a church or draconian rules or laws; there were no threats of hellfire and devils that would stick pitchforks in me if I didn't obey what they said.

I did commit to getting out of bed every morning before 5:00 a.m. to meditate and I did that for many years every day, not missing one day. My spiritual life became very important to me and the search for a meaningful practice was on. The entire time that I was on my spiritual quest, I can only consciously recall hearing about Kundalini from one teacher, and I later found out he didn't actually know too much about it. I read this man's book and went to see him several times. I even met with him at one point. Again, my inner guidance system is very rarely wrong; something seemed off the boil with him. Years later, I read an online interview in which he confessed to being a "fake guru" (his words) who was conning himself and other people who believed him and were following him around, worshipping him (people love to have someone to follow). He also talked about his own major struggles with alcoholism and drug addiction whilst playing guru.

* * *

There have been many highs and lows during my time in the States. Before coming to America, if I had been shown on a big screen what lay ahead of me or how certain people were going to treat me in the end, I might not have left. But I never had the luxury of seeing my future. People had promised me that no matter what happened they would remain on my team but when the circumstances changed the same people changed with the circumstances . . . or *had* they really changed? Or was it just that their true colors eventually were revealed. As mentioned previously, the truth always comes out in the end. Maybe they had no integrity to begin with. Yet on some level no doubt I knew that intuitively—and as always I ignored the truth and paid the price, so I can't blame anyone for anything. Lessons learned.

I have learned that I'm a good person who has a great strength to continue fighting and keep going under intense pressure; maybe that's the Celtic blood in me. I stand for what I believe in and have faced everything that has come my way. I have tried to do it with honesty and integrity. Those aren't common qualities in today's society I have found—but my journey is mine and yours is yours, and I respect that. But that doesn't always make for a fair go at life. Life just doesn't seem fair a lot of the time, and I don't think it's supposed to be.

Countless times I have questioned God and asked him why I'm being dealt the cards I seem to be getting; sometimes the same cards over and over again. However, in hindsight, some great force within me and even in my messiest moments made sure I had what I needed to stay in the game. At times the goods weren't delivered until one minute to midnight, as I waited anxiously. Other times I felt abandoned by this force, and worse, I went through dry, dark spiritual deserts when I questioned whether this protective force I call God even existed. (Boy do I see this different today!) At times I didn't think I could go through any more struggles and there were many moments along the way when I just wanted to lie down and die for I could find no peace in my life. Sometimes peace can only be found in the struggle.

This brings me to the final stretch of my story and perhaps the darkest period of it all—but in a wonderful way and on a different level it seems like the journey is really only beginning. For I have come to learn that the awakening is only the beginning of the journey—not the end—I had it the other way around.

* * *

I had been looking to get out of my career as an ironworker for quite some time. I was constantly thinking about what I could do with my life instead of this tough work in this weak condition. My heart yearned to be doing what my soul's next call of duty was. I knew I wasn't fulfilling what I came here to do, not all of it anyway—but I just couldn't take the next step. I didn't know how to. Since the exorcism and Kundalini awakening, not to mention the accidents I had picked up on the job, I had clearly struggled to stay in that career.

It had been quite a few years since this battle had begun. I quietly hustled every day just to keep my head above water and food on my table. I had missed a nice chunk of time from work through my ordeals. I looked forward to the weekends and holidays just so I could have a day or two off to lie down and rest or maybe have a deep massage to help my aching body. That's what my life had become—looking to get a rest whenever I could.

I couldn't shake the fatigue or the muscle aches in my legs and my body hurt most days. The Kundalini had really done a demolition job on me and left my body and nervous system in a hell of a state. Most of the time I didn't know how to work with it. I wasn't prepared or expecting its arrival you might say, and I definitely hadn't fully healed yet. Nor did I have any real guru to guide me. I still feel this at times even today, given that so much energy has rushed through my system and caused major stress to it. I don't know if I will ever heal fully but I'll certainly continue to look for answers.

I remained unbalanced in large part because I was going into an environment every day that no longer served me. I couldn't continue to be defiant and go against the flow of the Kundalini energy for there would be a price to pay for not taking its guidance. This would be a big mistake on my end. The Kundalini energy can only be ignored for a while but it will always get your attention. That's what it has done with me, and I have learned to surrender to it more and more, always getting results when I can do that.

I didn't have many attractive options to turn to. I wasn't wealthy. I didn't have anyone to take care of me. I had lived alone for a long time and had battled through this whole nightmare practically alone. I wasn't receiving any kind of free handouts or feeling entitled that I should, for that matter. There comes a time, though, in this type of experience when you have to really start paying attention or things can get really dangerous. I had accumulated a number of worksite injuries: to my lower back, shoulder, and my neck, all of which had been injured within the space of a few years. These injuries didn't include the pulls, strains, nips, and burns I had suffered through. Even my leg had been crushed.

Was the universe trying to talk to me again? Was it trying to get me out of the construction field and open me up to something completely different? After all, some of the gifted Intuitive's and psychics I had worked with told me that some kind of holy service was in my future. Indeed, I *had* gotten involved in helping other people and I was passionate about it. I knew I had some healing gifts, and since the Kundalini had arrived, I knew that they had been brought to a different level. At times I questioned whether or not the healers I had worked with were just trying to perk me up and give me something to hang onto in my times of darkness by telling me that this was all leading me into the healing arena. Was it all just spiritual mumbo jumbo that didn't amount to anything at the end of the day? I couldn't deny all the experiences that were unfolding—something was taking place and I couldn't deny that part. That can be tricky though when you don't have anyone around you to validate and encourage you the same way they would if you were planning on going to law school for instance. Telling people that you are going to become a healer brings about strange looks in the West, because people like to limit you to their own little world. The truth is, however, that when you grow into trusting your own process more and more, the less validation you need from anyone, for you are able to believe that everything is happening according to divine order much of the time.

On many levels it would prove difficult to leave my union job in New York, for it offered more security than most jobs—especially to the ironworkers. It also had great medical benefits, pay, and security fund, and was represented by a great leadership who were always very kind to me. On top of all this, I was working for one of the top companies in the field; I held the position of foreman and as such, received extra money. I had done quite well financially, although at this point I had gone through all my savings twice, trying to get help and surviving the onslaught of the previous years, given everything that had happened. The life savings that I had worked very hard for were gone and the new little nest egg was dwindling fast.

These were some of the obstacles of my predicament, and truth be told, I never would have walked away from that job unless some golden opportunity had landed on my lap—I was too afraid. Life normally doesn't serve opportunities up to me on a silver spoon. Instead, they generally arrive looking like misfortune has struck. There are better lessons in the latter scenario although my ego wishes I didn't have to learn them.

The job was a cash cow for me and I wasn't ready to relinquish my grip so easily despite what was coming from my lips. I really tried to make it work and that was like wrestling with an alligator most days. Abdi used to ask me why I couldn't give myself any credit for how I carried and conducted myself the whole way through a situation that would have killed most people. I didn't have an answer but I thought about his question a lot. I realized that in the recovery program, we had been taught to not give ourselves credit for too much of anything. Abdi pointing this out to me made me realize that I did deserve some acknowledgment for what I had been through, and in this, I learned to be more gentle with myself.

Sometimes when things were really tough for me, both physically and mentally, I found myself envying the guys that I worked alongside, for life seemed to be relatively normal for them. I would listen to how trivial some of their problems were, and think, *Wow is he really making such an issue out of the same shit every day?* I know people have real problems but at least they could share them with each other and not be viewed as a freak. My shit wasn't coffee-break conversation, nor was it a topic fit for a recovery meeting. I struggled with the need to find someone who would understand my situation. Maybe I thought if I found that it would help set me free and I would no longer need to be understood. I can't imagine the reaction the Kundalini phenomenon would have received from the other ironworkers, or even a mention to them that I'd had an exorcism performed on me. They were completely oblivious to what I was going through.

Most of my friends and family, as well as my mentor, didn't know the whole story, either—what I was *really* going through behind closed doors. Only a handful of healers ever knew the whole story. For the most part, I had learned to process my own stuff by myself. However, when I could afford to or when I really needed to, I would reach out to someone in the healing community for help.

* * *

In 2015 and 2016, every day I would, along with my work colleagues, descend into the subway tunnel far underneath the ground. We were building the new Second Avenue subway station in New York City. I had gone from the top of the World Trade Center to underneath Second Avenue in a few years—talk about getting pulled in different directions! Only an ironworker could make something like that happen! As always, my union came up with the goods by giving me a good job. I had worked for this company for a year and a half and had done a previous job with them—I was on a run you might say. I liked the company and was trying to get ahead and save some money and get my health back in order. I had just come back from a two-week vacation in Ireland—I had been there for the holidays. I was in a really dark funk, I had been for some time. It was a strange place, a dark lifeless place; nothing in life seemed to have any value. However, I was trying to be patient and let things settle and integrate.

My trip to Belfast had brought the strangest experience to

me. I had felt very alone there—as if I had lived in the place in a different lifetime. It was obvious I didn't fit in there anymore and now the new man that I had become couldn't find his place in life. It was like being stuck between two countries, or actually, like being stuck between two different worlds: the mundane world that was once the only world I knew, and now the strange mysterious world of the Kundalini that needed integration. It was dark and confusing, and loneliness was with me despite being surrounded by my family. But I have always really been on my own. Even with all the friends and family I have in my life, I've always felt that void.

I walked down all the old streets I used to play on, past the bars I used to drink in, and across the football fields I used to play on, just to see if I could ignite a spark and get life flowing again. But there was nothing. I travelled over to Scotland on the ferry to watch my beloved Celtic play in Glasgow, for I used to be so excited to do that. However, I still felt like a dead man who just hadn't stopped breathing yet.

I later came across some writings and the knowledge that I was in between a place of death and rebirth when the karma from past lifetimes and this one are coming from the depths of the psyche, cleansing and healing it so that the soul can make the transition beyond suffering. In the spiritual circles I was searching I couldn't find anyone who knew about this place; it's a rare point on the journey. You can try anything you want to get out of this place that I can only describe as hell, but it's like being in a maze, and you can't leave it until it's time to leave it. I had even read in the classic text, *The Tibetan Book of the Dead*, that some souls get stuck in this hell or similar hells and never leave them.

The only place I could gather my thoughts every day was in the chapel. As we know, I hadn't exactly been a devout Catholic my whole life to that point, but there was something about sitting in a chapel in Belfast that I loved. I typically experience a peaceful, higher vibration when I enter an old holy building. My father would drop me in town each day and I would walk into the church through its big wooden doors and look up at the nice paintings and windows inside.

I would look around the chapel as people would come and go, light candles, and pray. My granny would do the same thing in that chapel for me and everyone else when she was alive. My granny is hands down the most inspiring authentic practicing Catholic and beautiful loving human being I have ever witnessed, she had her hands full for most of her life. I noticed that everyone that passed through the church seemed to have suffering on their faces and no one was smiling as they entered God's house. It was easy for me to see that they were all looking for some help for something greater than themselves.

I knew that people in that part of the world had suffered quite a bit and I wished I could create some kind of a shift for each of them, to bring them some peace, but I didn't even seem to be able to do that for myself. Outside the church I noticed that the winos on Castle Street had got much younger since I was a kid, and were now accompanied by many homeless East European immigrants who lay on the ground outside the shops with blankets wrapped around them, begging for money.

* * *

I experienced a deep sense of hurt and pain when I left Belfast, which made me feel as if I was submerging into a dark hole day-by-day. On the plane ride back to New York I was deeply distressed because once again I was leaving everything I had once known and loved. Life didn't make sense to me anymore. I didn't understand the ways of it, or where it was leading me to. It was clear to me that I had to walk my path alone and that no one could save me from it but myself.

My return to New York in January 2016 was full of emptiness. I felt like a lost soul; I just couldn't figure it all out and the best I could come up with was that I had gone back to Belfast to let go of that part of my past completely and to be shown were I now was on my journey. I'm not saying that I was cutting my ties with my family and friends because that will never happen. Instead it felt as though I was burning off more karma. My trip back to Belfast was a marker of sorts on my mysterious and unpredictable journey. It had shown me where I was at, which wasn't pleasant for I didn't like what I was seeing and feeling.

Home again in New York I felt isolated like never before. The feeling that everything was dying wouldn't go away. Not only had I struggled to stay in my job, but I had struggled to stay in the recovery community after the Kundalini had hit full force, even after some of my spiritual guides had suggested I was done there. As discussed earlier, being so open energetically was as if I had access to everyone else's pain and suffering in the recovery meetings. This was really damaging me and having a detrimental effect on my well-being. In many of the meetings I attended, a lot of the people there didn't really want to get well and were putting on a big show, pretending like they were on some great path, but I could see and feel the energy and actions were unauthentic.

I would be super consciously aware of people who were hiding their real issues. Coupled with this was the fact that not everyone in the recovery circles I attended was trying to live a spiritual way of life. I also struggled with the fact that more and more people who didn't belong in that community seemed to be taking it over and having a big say in the running of the meetings. They had found a place to break their loneliness or use the meetings as a form of therapy for their narcissism, which they categorized as alcoholism.

In the past I had been able to see this on the surface level, but now being around these people was becoming a real problem for me. As my awakening unfurled, this extreme opening in my whole sensory system allowed me to sense very easily, just by looking at someone, if they were hiding behind their issues. I think a large majority of people I have met actually don't want to get well or grow spiritually. They just want their toys back or they want to get new toys and/or to have their own way—that's why most of them will stay asleep and continue to suffer. I had such a different and more beautiful experience with people who were really looking for help and wanted to get well. No matter how dark and broken they were it would be a great help to me to help them!

Still, much of it was exhausting. Even listening to the talks and the stories in the meetings was boring me as my heart wasn't in it and it would pain me, both physically and psychologically, to try and sit through the discussions. It felt like my soul had left the place two years previously but the body just hadn't followed yet. Again, as I had experienced on my recent trip to Belfast, it seemed like I just didn't fit in anymore. I would go to meetings every night and try to turn the volume and ferocity of my program up as loud as I could, to see if my situation would change, but my condition only worsened.

Every time I would attend a meeting I'd leave sick, for I would have taken on everyone's energy. At times I would get into arguments and confrontational situations with people who I could see were phony. I wasn't feeling self-righteous at all; it wasn't like that. It's more that I was stunned and trying to protect myself given that I would feel under attack from the energy that the posers and predators in that community were displaying. Obviously not everyone was like this, but a decent amount of folks were. I couldn't help but react, but then I would have to go back and apologize to them. Other times people would ask me for help but I knew they weren't sincere about it and I would have to eventually get away from them or they would move on from me which I would welcome.

Today, now that I'm grounded, I know that what's going on with other people is not my business. I also am able to use discernment as to who comes into my space. If they choke me up or bring darkness, I side step aside quickly. I have to. I also give folks the benefit of the doubt and will try to give time to or help anyone who needs it; thank God *that* changed for me. I fully understand that I am no better than anyone and that everyone is where they are on their journey. That said, I don't have to get into someone's dream world with them either. Back then I didn't have protective tools at my disposal, especially when the Kundalini was charging up my body and clearing the blockages. At these times, it removed the boundaries between other people and me. I know everyone is doing the best with what they have. I'm not judging anyone here, just relaying how things played out for me.

In any event, my reaction to this new way of living must have looked very strange to others at times. Part of the problem I had being around anyone inauthentic was due to the fact that I had been forced to work through my own stuff on a deep level and a super cleanse had taken place within me and my system at a frantic pace. As a result, I couldn't tolerate anything toxic, cheap, or dishonest so easily. This proved to be disorientating and I would go home from meetings wondering way I even bothered going. At times I would be disturbed for hours, as my body and mind would try to cleanse themselves of everything I'd picked up in the meeting that day.

Don't misunderstand what I'm saying here. I really tried to ignore what was happening with me, and asserted myself by trying to act the way I had in the past. But that didn't feel natural and I was clashing with it big time. I knew I had to do something quickly or suffer. Perhaps I should just quit recovery all together. I knew that I had to find my own answers given that my life seemed to be slipping away from me bit by bit. Or was it that my ideas about how my life should look were slipping away?. . . Either way I was being forced to play my cards and make some moves.

Thus I began to tell my circle of friends and even told my mentor and sobriety linage that I was calling it a day and would be moving on from the recovery meetings. Some of my friends were very upset and my mentor had some choice words to say on the matter. That part was the most difficult as he had been such an instrumental part of my journey and was a great man with wonderful wisdom and insights into life. He didn't want things to end this way, nor did I. What I really wanted was to be able to fit back in but it seemed like my work there was finished.

I understood a lot of the dynamics of the situation. I also knew that the pushback I received was because these people cared about me and didn't want to see me heading for trouble. I understand that if one makes the wrong decision in this situation it can prove fatal. Specifically, I know people who have left recovery to follow different spiritual paths like the church, and they got took up drinking again instead.

But my wanting to leave wasn't about the church. I had activated Kundalini and was having a very deep awakening, so deep it would have freaked most people out if I'd shared the truth of it with them. How could I explain to people that my whole being had been rewired? But that's the truth and it happened to me and to others I have met along this path: Kundalini changes everything. I felt like a phony not being able to speak my whole truth to people that were close to me out of fear of being viewed as crazy, I had to find a way to honor my truth.

Be that as it may, what I had really started to do was to cut people out of my life that cared about me and loved me. At this point, the darkness started to thicken and overwhelm me in a very scary way. I got the vibe that I was heading further into an extremely dark tunnel, which was the weirdest feeling ever.

I couldn't dodge the fear, or the feeling of being dazed, confused, and disconnected from life anymore. Was this complexity and darkness going to continue until my last breath or would I be able to find peace again? One of my teachers is an ex-Buddhist monk. John had once been in a 12-step fellowship himself and had left for reasons that were similar to mine for leaving. At times it could take up to a month to get an appointment to talk to him. On this particular day, I reached out to his secretary and asked when would be the quickest meeting I could have with him, given that my situation was urgent. She emailed me back within ten minutes informing me he had just received a cancellation for that afternoon. This was one of those divinely inspired moments where a higher intelligence was at work. It was so clear to me that I was being taken care of that day.

After speaking with my teacher and explaining my story, he

pointed out that the darkness had gotten thicker when I started to cut people out of my life. He typically would ask me to sit with myself and ask myself questions so that I would find my own answers. In this case, he advised me to sit and feel, within my own body, what ending my recovery practice might feel like.

After I'd been sitting for a time the answer that came to me was "love." That's what life is always about he replied, no matter where we are on life's journey or what strange or different experiences we are having. He told me to open my heart and let those people back in, and in that moment I knew I had some phone calls to make. It sounds pretty straightforward but this stuff needed to be pointed out to me as I actually couldn't see it. He told me that I was really effective in the recovery groups. He went on to say it appeared that I had enjoyed myself most of the time in that fellowship. It had given me so much, hadn't it? Basically everything. When I really examined the issue, I realized that he was right. Why would I leave? I got what I needed from our conversation and thanked him and left.

I valued what he had said, given that he had a long history with Kundalini himself.

I also knew that I would have to find a way to reconnect in that environment in a healthy way if I was going to stay in it. I reconnected with my friends, my mentor, and all of my buddies. And for the most part I am in a better place with it. I don't leave exhausted most of the time. I have found a much better way of not taking unbearable, unwanted energy into my field, wherever I go. I don't really pay much attention to anything other than trying to be a part of the process and to be of service. If I get a sense of darkness from someone, or the feeling that I shouldn't stay around that person, then I don't—not for too long anyway. I'm glad I got through that phase of being so open and crippled by other people's stuff, which was a real handicap and a nightmare for me at times. Learning to stay present in the midst of adversity is a real gift, and apparently something that I needed to learn as part of my healing journey.

Chapter 12
The Universe Forces My Hand Once More

In working on the subway job under the streets of New York, the air quality was terrible and I got sick many times as result. I noticed that the rest of the crew would get sick regularly also. I would argue with the safety guy all the time, citing the need for better conditions for the men. He didn't give a fuck about the men—he was just there representing the general contractor to keep down their insurance premiums, a total act. When I would go home at night and get into the shower, I would spit black soot out of my mouth and pick the dirt out of my nose. It was like going into a living hell every day even though the men I worked with were all good guys on this job and we had our laughs. This wasn't a place activated Kundalini wanted to dwell, given that it was dark, dingy, dusty, and there were rats everywhere.

It was a super freezing New York winter's day when I made that descent into the bowels of Manhattan for one of the last times. The universe was going to take my door off its hinges once again in yet another attempt to get my full and undivided attention. On that particular day, I was dressed well, with plenty of extra layers on, but I could still feel the cold through everything. I recall I was having a tough day energetically and was struggling to walk with the fatigue and soreness in my joints and body—it was if I had two twenty-pound weights strapped to each leg. On days like this I had to really dig in and use everything I had just to get over the finish line to the day's end, at which point I would go home and collapse on my bed.

One of the guys working on a different detail was trying to get me to help him with what he was doing. I had been busy and told him no on three separate occasions but he persisted. He was a young guy and also a friend, so I eventually gave in and agreed to help him out. I put on a harness and went up twenty-five feet on a lift to install a piece of steel. I lifted the length of steel by hand and tried to drop it into place. The platform I was on was cluttered with all kinds of mess and I tripped and lost my balance. The weight of the piece pulled me down with a great force, finally twisting me and snapping my neck.

Instantly I knew that some serious damage had been done. It was freakish, and for the next few days the pain escalated into excruciating torture. I awoke on that Saturday morning at 5:00 a.m., finding it hard to articulate in words what I felt. My neck was frozen stiff, and the pains shooting out of it and radiating down my left arm and into my hand were agonizing. I couldn't get out of bed and in a state of pain and intense discomfort I didn't know what to do or where to turn. I couldn't think straight as I lay there groaning to myself for some time. It was extraordinary.

Suddenly I remembered a chiropractor who had once helped me and, getting online, I found out that his office was open on Saturday. I took myself there and waited outside in the freezing cold until his office opened. It was the coldest day of the year and that wasn't helping my case at all.

Eventually I saw the doctor and he basically told me there was nothing he could do. He sent me for an MRI that day, telling me I'd have to wait a few days for the results. After the MRI I was in so much pain that, under the instruction of a friend, I landed in the emergency room on Sunday afternoon. Waiting to be called in to see the ER doctor, I was bent over with pain in the waiting room. I recall coming to when I was called by a nurse who was shouting out my name. I'm not sure how long I had passed out for. Thank god it was obvious to them I wasn't doing well and they rushed me right in to the doctor without making me fill out a bunch of paperwork. After a few questions, he shot me up with a non-narcotic painkiller, and then prescribed some heavy-duty drugs for me, which I was a little concerned about taking.

I had to be cautious with the narcotics. I had heard the horror stories of people in recovery misusing drugs and ending up in big trouble, although a couple of painkillers never produced the same effect on me as a few shots whiskey or vodka did. I actually didn't take the narcotics until later that night when I was really feeling the pain again. Thankfully I used them wisely. When the chemicals were unleashed in my body, they made me feel sick, as if my system was rejecting them. I have no way to explain why they made me feel sick. However, there had been so many changes within my inner workings, especially in the nervous system and the subtle body. This was a result of the Kundalini having transformed everything, shifting my body and consciousness to many different levels as a result of my multiple body refurbishments. I sensed that I was poisoning myself with the drugs but I wasn't complaining as I had been exhausted and was in great need of sleep and relief. And they did help to bring the pain level down.

After a few days I stopped taking the pills because they had ceased to do any good.

* * *

he next few months were unexpected and amongst the toughest I have ever had to endure in nearly every way. Having nothing but time on my hands, I sat around all day, immobile, and felt like I had nowhere to turn. My mind started coming at me with interesting stories—tales to the tune that I would never heal from this injury or come out of the dark hole I seemed to be going further into, and feeling like I had been stuck in it forever. I began to think I was living in a human torture chamber.

The physical pain joined with the mental chatter, not to mention the anxiety that my body was overcome with. I had lived a lot of my life avoiding looking within myself. I had used the job, the money, the girls—and all of the other material riches of this world that I could get my hands on such as booze and drugs—to distract myself. As previously mentioned, I even gave marriage a try for a short period, but being settled and starting a family wasn't my answer either. When you aren't right inside, nothing seems to work—when you're not the right guy there is no such thing as the right girl. Clearly, I was at a place where I totally knew nothing "out there" would cut it for me anymore.

I had worked with different meditations and different practices over the years and that got me to look within somewhat. However, it's so easy to fall into the trap of hiding behind spiritual practices and spirituality as another way to hide from yourself and the truth, whether those practices are the 12 steps or the path of Zen. Even using service as a way to hide from that anxiety whilst appearing to the world to be a humble servant is another way that the crafty ego tends to try and trick us.

What was about to occur would take me to levels way beyond any place I had ever seen or visited within myself. At different times of my awakening I had been taken to similar places and seen different visions—but not to this degree. It would feel as if the universe had kidnapped me and put a big pistol to my head and forced me to follow it down the darkest tunnel for the next period of time. I was pushed and sucked further and further down a winding staircase by the Kundalini—into the basement of my very own soul. It blasted open the hidden dungeon's doors and acquainted me with things I had been running from my entire life. This included the fake rationalization and the phony ideas about who I thought myself and everyone else to be. It became very obvious that I'm not truly this personality called Adrian and all the different aspects of that, which I had been obsessed with. It was all an illusion. My beliefs about life and myself had been hidden in the crevasses of my mind and soul, hiding behind all the constructs of the ego.

It was extremely intense and it all got stirred up as I faced this madness, which continued to flash in front of me . . . the lonely solitude that I was in . . . the pain and disability I was in the clutches of . . . not being able to provide for myself . . . I felt weak and helpless and as if I had no control over any of it. The fear that I would remain this way wouldn't shift. It continued to roll through my mind's eye and wouldn't let up; it would even awaken me in the middle of the night from torturous nightmares. The idea that I should take matters into my own hand by ending my life would come to me from time to time but there was some-thing much more awake and alive behind it all that made those thoughts seem weak and invalid. Although the ego's voice didn't have the power it once did, it wasn't finished. I was trying not to perceive this as a slap in the face from life, given what I had been through, though I would view it that way occasionally.

I haven't ever experienced darkness such as this in my whole journey. The death of ego is basically like hell on earth and I had been watching it dissolve and shed its layers of delusion for quite some time. However, it always rebuilt itself and came back in a different disguise. This time, however, what I faced was unimag-inable and petrifying. The Kundalini brought me to visit the deepest most hidden parts of self and I watched them fragment, which created the strange and hopeless feeling I was experienc-ing. I had no one to talk to about this, for people would think I was crazy—or worse, they become crazy themselves and try to match parts of their life's experience with something they didn't know anything about. Some places you must go alone. No teacher or teachings can hold your hand—this place was beyond all that.

I feel for people who are in the midst of a full Kundalini awakening. Most of them have no place to turn to for help and thus remain silent about their condition for fear that they'll be viewed as lunatics. The truth is that it's a very rare experience, even though it's being talked about more and more. However, for those of you out there who are going through this, please know that you will find real help if you persevere!

A big reason why I wrote this book was to invite others to come forth and reveal what's happening to them. I didn't want them to suffer in silence, I know I didn't want to sit back in the corner being isolated and not sharing this great gift I have been given with the world, although my ego would have had me do that. I'm glad I didn't listen to it or hold back information and write this book in a way I think I would like certain other people to see it in order to protect some image they might have about me.

How do you know if you are going through a genuine Kundalini awakening? I would go as far as saying if you didn't go through at least a year or two of total mayhem it's probably not Kundalini. I'm sure there might be exceptions to that, for I have also learned that anything is possible. I have met people who claimed they had been given Shaktipat by a holy man or guru and had prepared to receive a Kundalini awakening for years. (Shaktipat is the process by which spiritual energy is conferred onto one person from another.) I was skeptical with a lot of these people as most of them never seemed to go through any trauma or difficulties in their process and I couldn't relate to that. My Kundalini came in like a wrecking ball and took me apart at the seams bit by bit and then stitched me back together with a totally different system.

Certain authors who have written about Kundalini have asked me to comment or write a testimonial for their book. However, in the past I have declined because I was sure that what they were going through was not a genuine Kundalini awakening. I have met many people who have had an experience that lasted one day, or a situation that went on for a week or so. It might have been nice and made a fantastic shift, and I'm certainly not undermining that, but I have discovered that's not how Kundalini seems to work. That said, I know it works differently for everyone.

I reached out to my trustworthy guide Abdi for advice. I had visited him many times and in many rough states, but this was to be a very memorable visit for me. I explained what was happening, and as always he got it. I knew when someone got it by the way in which they would interact with me and the language they would use. I had started to realize that I was kind of getting it myself for I had developed a razor-sharp intuition. I have always been an intuitive but this was now on a whole different level of sharpness, awareness, and connectedness.

I would visit Abdi to have some non-hysterical, outside sane perspective and just to make sure I wasn't going mad, and to get some direction on what to do. I had gained better clarity at deciphering my stuff and using discernment about who to bring it to/share it with. Even though I knew there was way more involved in the spiritual journey than just the 12-step recovery community, I had personally limited the power of God and what can happen on the spiritual journey. I had judged it all with a finite mind.

It was clear that I had to stop talking about my experiences with people who had not gone through what I'd been going through. With that being said my recovery mentors were very important to me. They kept me in check and still do to this day. There is a lot of value in that that I can't find anywhere else.

* * *

In addition to my recovery group, I had accumulated a nice crew of healers, psychics, and shamans, some of them self-realized beings; I had become friendly with some of them. Through my healing, and as a result of waking up more and more, I began to see that these people were also indeed very human and there were aspects of their own personalities that hadn't been healed. I'm talking about people who had real powers—powers that could change someone's life in a huge way just by laying their hands on that person's head. So without judgment and being very grateful for the work that I was able to do with them, I knew it was time to move on and close those doors. If you are on a serious spiritual journey, invariably the time comes when you have to stand on your own two feet and stop running to everyone seeking their advice and approval. You have to start to really trust and listen to yourself. When this time comes you'll know it.

I have learned a lot from different healers and the different ways healing may be accomplished. I have also learned that the most powerful healers and teachers can have a darkness and craziness to them that's a totally different side to their powers. A lot of them never seem to do the healing work on their own personalities and I have found different reasons for that. Some just aren't aware of it, others think they are too high and mighty and divine to need to change their ways or the ways of their inflated ego. I have seen that a person can be "enlightened" and still be an asshole.

I have always trusted Abdi. He never steered me wrong and in all of my interactions with him he projected professionalism. He was also very warm and a great healer. We grew up in different parts of the world but had a lot in common. We had similar obstacles on each of our paths—I think we connected on a street level as well as a spiritual one. Isn't it ironic that I would trust some folks on the street more than some of the self-proclaimed teachers or even the authors who have written best-selling books? I have also found that some of my friends and family have a lot more integrity than these people.

When I spoke to Abdi on that particular day I told him that it had been a long time since I had been in a similar type place to this. He abruptly pointed out to me that I had never been in a place like this before. That was a pretty good call actually, for what he said was spot-on: I hadn't ever before felt or experienced this place that I was brought to visit, although I had been used to pain and darkness.

At that point I had a sense that I knew what he was about to say next. He told me that my hand had definitely been forced by the universe so that I could move to the next place. He also told me to not to be concerned, for I was being protected. Apparently this was all part of the unfolding.

It's tough to believe that when it seems like everything is being stripped away from your life. In the past I was able to go to the gym or find some form of physical activity to distract myself when things got crazy. However, these fallback activities were no longer viable given my serious neck injury. Everything that I had ever believed myself to be had been taken away or seriously challenged and walls that my ego had cleverly constructed over a lifetime and imprisoned me behind had been dissolving, leaving me fully exposed and vulnerable in the process.

The dissolution of my ego had been happening for a few

years at this point, meaning that most of the desires and the self-centered things that used to motivate me had totally disappeared and no longer mattered. Not all of them, but a lot of them. This left me feeling disorientated as I was observing it all unfold. I don't want to be claiming I understood what was taking place but I sure got a strong sense about it. The Kundalini appeared to be an intelligent force that knew exactly what it was doing. Abdi advised me to step back and let the process have its own way, to surrender to it all and let it unfold. I didn't have a choice for it felt like my ego was being bullied and dragged about by the Kundalini; it was fighting for its life.

This was a very challenging part of the process and while it was clear to me that total surrender was required, I wasn't having much of a say in it all. It seemed like the process was doing *me*. My perception of awakening has drastically changed and at times I would rather have died than continued on. There was nothing glamorous about it as I had naively believed from what I had read in some books and based on what a lot of people I listened to over the years had said.

I would say to anyone who would listen, don't forcefully try to raise your Kundalini because you've heard about the wonderful blissful effects and states that it can have or because you want to copy someone else. It can be an absolute living hell, and you can't ever reverse it and go back to the life you once lived. I'm not saying don't raise it, but only do so if you are seriously sure that you want to go deeper on your journey and on your spiritual path. And if you do it, do it with a reputable teacher who knows what they're doing and one who will inform you of the high risks involved. Even with all that being said, there's no guarantee you will actually raise the Kundalini. I have spoken to people who have sought it for years and haven't got near it.

I have met girls and guys here in the States—some of them young and others older—who have promised people certain experiences in their Kundalini yoga classes. Some of them I have spoken to directly and they actually believe that they have activated their own Kundalini. I'm not saying they haven't, but when

I would share little parts of my experience with them and some of the madness that happened they would be alarmed and quite surprised. A person like this can't help you if the Kundalini comes roaring into your body and you end up with the Kundalini crazies. Instead, you will be on your own and a fluffy yoga class will be the last place where you will be able to find help.

* * *

I have learned that my spiritual journey has been one of healing. It's been about awakening to the parts of myself that needed to heal. The dark broken unresolved pieces of my soul were brought to the surface and into the light for healing. This was stuff from childhood and, people say, from past lives. I don't know if that process will ever be finished for me but I feel that it's got much softer. Facing the rising contents of my own psyche and the shadows of the subconscious is not easy but there became a time when it just couldn't be ignored anymore. It was time to work through it all and this has been my time to do this work. The Kundalini created that opening into the soul. No more distracting myself with life's toys and ambitions, neither could I suppress what wanted to come forward. Avoidance causes blocks which prevents awakening and freedom. It seems like the journey has been the subtraction of illusions on the path home to the True Self, or the falling away of the beliefs and a resolving of the old issues.

The Kundalini sped that process up into full throttle for me so much so that at times it was like sitting on a Kundalini roller-coaster heading back home, smashing through the walls of illusion along the way. Anytime I was in great fear or pain, when I didn't have faith that the universe knew what it was doing—which came on different levels for me and of course deeper surrenders—having faith was key.

This was more easily said than done, however, as I was realistically facing the possibility of losing my apartment, my car, and my career. The past five years had taken all my savings and everything I had worked for and toward. I was trying to survive and find answers. It was crazy, the very thing that had created me and was one with me, had shown me every step of the way that it was providing for me and taking care of me! I felt I would be dropped at the next turn in the road many times. I'm only human after all. I sure hope if you are having a similar experience, dear reader, that you surrender a lot more quickly than I did. If not, it can be brutal.

* * *

On the Monday morning after my visit to the ER, the doctor called and said the results from my MRI were very bad and that I should make my way to his office immediately. When I got to his practice he sat me down, and lifting a plastic model of a cervical spine off his desk, he proceeded to show me its discs and bones. Then, from a sheet of paper, he began to read my MRI results to me. I couldn't really understand the fine details of the medical terms for body parts but I certainly got the gist of it, and it didn't sound good at all. There were three herniated discs. The worst were C-7 and C-6, covering the left foramina orifice. I deciphered the message of the medical lingo: my neck was in really bad shape.

When I got the news, my first reaction was fear. My first question was, How long will I be out of work? He told me to forget about work, and then informed me that he was sending me to a neurologist to be further examined.

I was in total shock. Professionally, I had been having a decent run, the best I'd had in years. I had worked hard to get out of the red and I had a good job. This was disastrous; at least that's what my mind was yelling at me. But sometimes God showed up with a sledgehammer when I was resisting something in some area of my life. Apparently I needed to be moved along, so I got a little nudge—a painful little one.

The universe couldn't have shouted my name any louder. "Adrian, do you really want leave this job and find a different way of life, do something different?" It asked me. Consider it done! But it wasn't like I had any real choice in the matter. Be careful what you ask for. At the end of the day I didn't really know what was good for me. Sometimes the greatest gifts come in a disguise of what looks to be sheer misfortune. As I've covered my face in dismay and peeked through my fingers, I've seen flowers grow and bloom out of the dirt and destruction of what appears to be a mishap.

I walked over to the neurologist's office that day in the rain. I felt lost and was feeling sorry for myself, almost in victim mode. The neurologist confirmed that I had a very serious neck injury and it was highly possible that I would need surgery. What I find ironic is that all three of my main injuries happened right along the chakra line of my spine—right where the Kundalini flows upward.

I was convinced that the energy helped heal my previous two injures but this one seemed a lot more serious. I was put on a course of steroids and all kinds of tests were carried out on me over the next while for the numbness, pain, and tingling that I was constantly feeling. In the forefront of my mind all I wanted to do was return to work. I'm programmed that way. So I asked the doctor about that. He wanted to know what type of work I did and when I told him, he said that with the severity of the injury I had, I wouldn't be able to return to work for a very long time. This was not what I wanted to hear and my ego was spinning, calculating how much money I was losing out on as we spoke, and how quickly the remainder of my savings would disappear if this didn't heal.

The ego's stories about this would all be dismantled very shortly. I also discovered that this doctor was letting me down gently. On my next visit with him I explained to him that the drugs he had given me had reduced the pain a considerable bit but they had made me really sick. This was two weeks after my first visit and even though I was better, the pain and numbness wouldn't go away. I asked him the million-dollar question one more time, "When can I return to work"?

He became rather frank with me as he tossed his pen onto his desk and replied. "Adrian, I'm going to be honest with you," he told me. "I'm marking this down as a career ending injury. You cannot return to that job with or without surgery. If you do, you will end up paralyzed."

I knew in my heart what he was telling me was true, but my mind still clung to the idea that I wasn't finished. I visited the surgeon and he clarified that I should have surgery, but a spinal fusion wasn't something I wanted to rush into. Having the threat of permanent disability made me take a close look at what was important in my life. Good health is a great thing to have and my health hadn't been good for quite some time. Life had continuously put me on the sidelines so that this Kundalini process could do its work. I had been blind to the great many gifts that I had been given and the magical wave that I had been riding for a while. I started to focus on that as the doctor helped me to surrender to the idea that my time as an ironworker was up.

I left his office that day with a sense of peace. Pain and all, I think I was believing, in reality, that the accident was part of the divine order of things that were being served up. Maybe something new was on the horizon—something great. I had many mixed emotions at this time. There was certainly a part of me that was looking forward to the next chapter and excited about my future. How could I have walked through everything that had happened and not believe that this universe or life had an intelligence that had my best interests at heart?

The darkness continued to hover, however, as did the fear about what was next. And despite all the evidence and synchronized events that had taken place, I still at times questioned whether or not a universal intelligence was mapping out my path and leading the way for me. I have struggled with this question for many years and, at different points on my journey—generally when the ego was just about to get sprung—this idea of no universal intelligence would show up. I have tried to pick the heads of enlightened beings on this matter. Some say yes there is a universal intelligence. Others say no there is not. I say we're all fucked if there's not. The truth is that, at the end of the day, this is something that you have to draw your own conclusions about.

At times of great fear and stress this question would always raise its head. And when it did, I would seek out spiritual books and practices to see if I could find the answer to this great mystery, for it's been super important to me. In the midst of all my struggles and the uncertainties about my life and my future, this question would wiggle its way in and push me into deep thought and reflection. I would pray and ask to be shown signs that I was indeed being taken care of. I had become used to that little prayer. ("Please make it obvious to me that you are taking care of me, universe.") Sometimes using it directly would bring direct results to me.

Around this time I received an email about a book on Kundalini, almost by chance. Anytime I see the word *Kundalini* I always read what's been written. Well, let's say I *begin* to read it. In this case, I noticed the email in my inbox right away, so I knew to pay close attention to it as I had become used to these direct synchronized events happening in my life. Still struggling with certain blockages and ailments in the body from the Kundalini and always looking for answers, I decided I would buy the book.

While I read the book I sensed that something felt off about it, like it had no heart and soul. However, I was very interested in a lot of the information I was reading and I could tell that there was good chance the author had indeed, experienced Kundalini. Some of the info seemed accurate and was definitely informative, even though he had done a lot of quoting about what others had said on the subject. I'm always skeptical when a book says more about what other people thought and said than what the author's actual experience is. Again, I sensed strongly that something didn't add up.

I was led to a second book on the same subject, with a different angle, by the same author. I thought, *What the hell let me read that one also*. Strangely, I had a deeper feeling that something was off with the second but still couldn't put my finger on what that was. Finding an email address in one of the books, I was strongly guided to send a letter, something that I never had done in the past.

One thing led to another and to my surprise, through the author's secretary, I found myself on the other end of a phone conversation that lasted almost one hour. But five minutes into our talk I was able to pinpoint what I had previously deemed to be off about this man's books. He was an atheist. Yes, an atheist. He had lived with Kundalini in his body for over thirty years. The body was a test tube to him and he believed it was all one big science project. He also believed the Kundalini had an intelligence but was sure it was limited and definitely not divine. I was stunned in a way, but continued to listen to him as I processed my newfound information.

An atheist with Kundalini! I was interested in some of the things he had to say, given that much of it was right on point, including a discussion of the diet and how for anyone who was experiencing Kundalini, their living conditions might need to change. He knew the biological aspects of it very well. But I couldn't help but notice that he had a pop at religion and at what some of the ancient texts had deemed Kundalini to be. He was rubbishing what the ancients had said. He had at least three negative blasts at religion within five minutes at one stage, and went on about how religious fundamentalists are preventing science from really investigating the cosmic life-force. (He may have had a point there.)

I didn't need to ask him his opinion on the nonexistence of God; he thought it was a useless debate. Besides, I was getting a little bored with his supper intellectual metaphysical explanations for everything. He was a nice man, and it sounded to me like he had found a path that had worked for him. And apparently he had grounded his experience enough that he could live a long life in the process, and I respect that. But his beliefs or lack of beliefs about everything didn't make that much sense to me. I have nothing against atheists, but I do think it's a radical position in the same way I think religious fanatics can be radical.

* * *

At one point, I spent a short time out in North Dakota and crossed paths with some folks there who were totally obsessed with Jesus in a militant fashion. They followed me around half the night forcing their views upon me and informing me of what I had to do. They told me that I should have Jesus in my heart because I would go to hell if I didn't. (This caused a little déjà vu there.) Here was the universe clearly answering my prayers and showing me both sides of the question I had asked it over and over again. This was a question that had plagued me for most of my adult life.

I have to say my experience with the atheist was a more pleasant one than this one in North Dakota. I would definitely have chosen to spend time with him versus the drunk-on- Jesus approach. I have nothing against Jesus either. He holds a huge place in my heart, as does the Buddha and Allah; is there a difference in what they taught?

My inability to answer the question of what lay behind everything was a source of frustration for me. Was there a divine intelligence making things happen within a divine order or not? It's easy to say that a divine order exists when things are going your way. I have come to see that's not the real question, however. What I have really been searching for and asking is, Will I be secure and loved and provided for in this world no matter what happens, especially when it looks like my resources are failing? Anytime that the things I had put faith and trust in looked like they might be getting taken away, the fearful question would arise again. I would worry about being abandoned, or worse, I would think that perhaps there was nothing to abandon me.

Did we really come from anything? Are we evolving anywhere? Does the human experience and life mean nothing? My meeting the atheist was to clearly show me how agnostic I was in my life. The fact that a man can have Kundalini in his body and still not believe there is a God definitely stunned me, however, was I not saying almost the same thing as this man? My crisis of faith seemed as baffling as it had ever been. Facing surgery on my spine and coming very close to selling my possessions so I could pay my rent gave the question some extra power.

I never ever pondered this question when I was having my desires and needs met, when I was being fulfilled and gratified by the phony impermanent material pleasures of the physical world. I'm not saying I don't like nice things. I love nice things and I want to be comfortable. I would like to make lots of money. But I know that game is up, as far as bringing lasting peace and happiness.

I pondered everything that was taking place and asked myself, If an atheist was to ask me to prove that there is a God and to provide an explanation for this universe—what would my reply be? I didn't know, but eventually it came to me, and the answer's really simple: every step of my experience—that's my proof. I don't have anything other than that and no one can ever take it away from me. I look at what I have walked through in my life and how I still continue to keep going down this path. It has to be divinely directed and inspired. I know those are just words, but what's beyond the words has a great power.

I believe I'm a part of this divine intelligence, but I would always forget that or get confused by it when life got busy or tough. I was born awake and one with this universe and I can remember all of this—before the worldly conditions got slapped on me. Like the majority of people, I fell under the illusion of separation from the oneness when life began to happen. I believe every human being has been put on this earth with the potential and invitation to awaken to our true nature and return home. I love how one of my favorite teachers describes this as "running around in the hand of God looking for God." It's total genius and it certainly had me fooled, like it does most people. But there's knowing that, reading about that, talking about that, and then there is actually waking up to that fact and experiencing it for yourself.

* * *

The gentleman's secretary contacted me and informed me that the author was inviting me to have another conversation about Kundalini with him. I thanked her but I didn't feel it necessary as I felt he had helped me as much as he could. And he *had* helped me. I enjoyed the divine sense of humor in this interaction. God bringing the answer-seeking agnostic and the atheist together in the name of truth.

* * *

I held off on the surgery for as long as I could but the pain and difficulty I was experiencing were just too much for me to endure every day. I revisited the surgeon and we agreed to have my neck fixed. We shook hands and began to prepare for the operation. This would prove to be a frustrating experience as I had become embroiled in a battle with an insurance company that was doing everything in its power to stall my surgery, which it did for quite a few months.

This stress added to all the other stress going on in my life at the time. Everything seemed to be falling apart. I had no income, my savings were dwindling away, I was doubting if I would ever work again, and my career looked as if it was over. Something inside me wouldn't accept that all this was turning against me and my old way of life was becoming a thing of the past. Although I should have let go, I dug in. I called my union and the company I had formerly worked for to see if I could pick up some work, as injured as I was.

My lawyer and a good friend, Jim, both talked me out of this and I'm glad they did because matters wouldn't have ended well. It seemed like all was being stripped away in my life, inside and outside. Everything was being dismantled and decommissioned—falling apart it seemed. Or was it falling together? Was this a breakdown or a breakthrough? I had to trust and believe in the latter and that wasn't easy at times, given the stress involved. However, underneath everything that was happening, I could sense my iron spirit, which was unfazed by it all.

People would ask me how I was doing and I would tell them what was occurring in my life. At a certain point, though, I stopped sharing the details, given that most people would get very dramatic and negative, which wasn't helping my cause. I used to be programmed this way also: everything was viewed as negative and disastrous. I can't go there today, it brings me down, so I don't indulge in people's dream worlds with them, which generally pisses them of, or surprises them at least. Nor was I playing the role of the delusional spiritual hippie who was watching his life burn to the ground either, and pretending like everything was fine, even though it clearly wasn't. I had a few people in my corner who I would receive help and guidance from and I even took a job with my friend Mike and his company out in Denver for a few months. However, when that ended, I had to return to New York to have the surgery done.

Over the past few years I had experienced a lot of mayhem and terror from the Kundalini and from everything that had happened to me. My relationship with the world had changed so much. I was in fact a different person from when it all began, with major changes in my personality and even my appearance. I find it amazing that I had to nearly lose everything I had and not have a clue what was around the next corner. And yet out of the darkness and hopelessness, a solid bedrock of creativity was formed. It gave me the inspiration to write most of this book. An amazing flow of words would issue forth from me when I would sit down to write. I clearly have been empowered by the Divine to do whatever I want, but still in all it will take some time to fully grow into that truth.

On a rip-roaring search looking for the Divine, I have met myself. I don't really have words to describe that, but I'm not who I thought I was. What has revealed itself to me is, in all its wonder and awe, beyond words and concepts and is certainly not what I expected. It was marked by moments of grace, as evinced by the following example: I went for a walk one Sunday night, around the time that I had begun to make peace with my struggle for faith. I was totally minding my own business and can't remember what I was even thinking about but there was some deep thought pattern going on. All of a sudden there was a pop in my mind and head, and in that moment I saw that I was not separate from that which created everything. It was self-revealing, I was one with it, and in that "ONE" moment I was being exposed to what felt like a magical reunion with my higher self.

Then I recognized that there had been moments of this before, which was the most familiar thing. However, in the past, the moment had not been marked by the same clarity and abruptness. God didn't show up—I woke up! And I didn't have to die and leave my physical body and go somewhere in an afterlife for that to happen. What a blessing and healing this has all turned out to be! I have suffered a lot and spent many years wishing for a different experience, never happy with the one I had. And I wouldn't want to switch places with anyone today.

No matter what your life's circumstances are—never give up! Keep walking every day and ask the universe for help, then open your eyes and watch what will be delivered to you. Invariably it will be what you need. The age of awakening is very much with us and the idea or myth that you need to be a yogi meditating in some cave in the Himalayas to wake up has been more than squashed. My experience proves that. I know no matter what life looks like, I'll be safe and protected by the Divine. How can I not be? I'm part of it, and you are too.

Epilogue

I wasn't that apprehensive when I went into surgery. I was trying to look at it like a shamanic ceremony—a completion of an old way of life in a sense—for I was prepared to come out the other end and begin anew. I had to be fixed, for it felt that my life had been taken from me. I missed going to the gym, and I hated having limits on what I could and couldn't do. I was also very uncomfortable with my excess weight.

A lot of power and prayer went into that surgery with me, from all of my healers, teachers, and of course, my friends. They wanted to stay informed about what I was going through so that they could pray and send healing energy into the operating room with me. I must say, it truly worked, for I came through the surgery just fine.

I was, however, in a lot of pain for the first week or so afterward and I needed some help. When your life is tough you get to see who your real friends are, and I was grateful for their help. It's been a long time since I was in a position where I had to rely on others so much and I really appreciate what they did for me. I'm happy to say that I'm getting stronger every day and am getting my life back in order even though this is not happening as quickly as I'd like and the pains of my injury haven't totally gone away and some days it even feels like I'm going backwards.

Through my awakening and especially in the time after I was injured I had learned so much about myself—my fears, strengths, and weaknesses—and what I would like to do in the future. Not a week goes by without some poor soul contacting me who is in the throes of a very difficult Kundalini awakening or having trouble with their life or some different type of awakening process. It's always the same story: They are isolated and afraid and finding it very difficult to stay on the Western hamster wheel. Everyone around them thinks they have gone crazy, when the truth is they haven't. The people around them don't understand the process they're in, but they are far from crazy. My advice to these suffering souls is:

find different people to be around.

That's what I did. It can be really difficult and awkward to explain to someone that you are terrified because your brain feels like it's on fire with this mysterious energy that's surging up your spine, or that dark entities just won't leave you alone. I have learned that I have a gift in talking to these beleaguered people who, like I was, are so desperate for help. I have been able to assist them in getting grounded in their lives and to make use of their experience instead of being spooked by it or thinking they have been befallen by unfortunate circumstances. The truth is that they have been blessed beyond belief.

I had to learn how to figure out my very challenging situation myself. Exactly one year later from my dark visit to Belfast I returned there as my surgeon give me permission to fly after my surgery. I felt a great urge to go there and I didn't know why but I have become used to obeying my heart's urges. When I stepped off the plane in Belfast it felt like I was stepping into a new sense of power; I felt this instantly. It was good to be home; the grass looked green and the mountains looked high. There was a lightness to the place and an aura of joy around me as it all made sense.

It felt like I had never left and I was totally present as my dad drove me into town and dropped me off there. I entered the chapel and sat quietly, feeling a pervasive sense of peace. I watched people enter and light candles with a lightness about them. Some of them made eye contact and smiled at me, and I smiled back. This was such a different experience from the previous year. It was a defining phase of my awakening, for it was evident to me that I had really stepped further into my own power and a serious amount of integration and growth had occurred within the last year.

Why shouldn't I show others how I had found my way? Before I met the healers I came in contact with, I wished there had been someplace I could have gone to in New York City or some number I could have called to get the aid I needed and to find help more easily than I had—just someone to tell me what was going on and that I was going to be fine. Because of this lack, I have made this one of my goals today: to be in a position to carry forward what I have learned from my experiences and to be present for the many people who follow behind me on this path. Life has pushed me into this position of healer and helper. It wasn't my choice, but I'm growing into that role on a deeper level all the time. It's about what life wants from me as opposed to what I want from life.

Heaven knows, the world has plenty of corrupt bankers, politicians, terrorists, and otherwise shady people who are just out for themselves. We are in great need of true healers, helpers, and teachers on this earth, for there is a mass global awakening in motion today and it seems to be multiplying at an increasing rate.

People often ask me why I think my Kundalini was activated. Today I believe it's because I'd had so much trauma in my life that I came to a point where it seemed that I could never work through it alone. Thus was the Kundalini activated, stepping in to help me and cleanse me. This makes sense as it seems to be a pattern with a lot of the folks I counsel; they have unresolved trauma and usually lots of it.

Given all of this, I'm excited to see what the world will look like in ten years. Hopefully by then Western science and medicine will have fully recognized the phenomenon of Kundalini awakening in all of its different guises and manifestations. Ideally, adequate care facilities will have been set up to help people make sense of and integrate their Kundalini experiences and the journey they are on—one that can leave them terrified and living close to the poverty line, given that they may have lost the capacity to function in the life they once knew.

Maybe it's man's journey to eventually awaken, if not in this lifetime, perhaps in another. In any event, awakening to one's fullest potential appears to be a primary purpose of human existence. My message is loud and clear: No matter what level of pain you have experienced in your life or what you may feel burdened with—be it your social circumstances or any other set of circumstances you find yourself in—never give up trying to find peace within, because in your true essence you *are* peace and so much more. Underneath everything I had to face and endure, there always seemed to be an iron spirit that kept driving me forward and wouldn't let me give up. And

I never did. Perhaps that's due to my Irish stubbornness but more so my passion to live.

As a result of experiencing the Kundalini, and indeed my whole awakening process, my consciousness has expanded greatly and continues to do so. As my awakening continues to unfold, it has brought me to a high vibrational frequency. I have been given a greater awareness of life, and access to deep spiritual insights that I could never have ever imagined before—a connection to a divine inner reality and a clear connection to the universal oneness that I'm but a small part of. The body and the mind have come into a greater sense of harmony with these energies and this awakened state, to the point where I feel that life should always have been this way. That said, each step along the journey has had a purpose and not one single bit of suffering has been in vain. Peace has found its way through to me and, along with that, a clarity and a freedom that I could never have dreamed possible.

Today I'm excited about the infinite possibilities before me and I am looking to be of service in this great universe that is home to us all.

Appendix: The Seven Chakras

1) Root Chakra – Foundational chakra
   Location: Tailbone at the base of the spine
   Emotional Issues: Basic issues of survival including monetary as well as food and shelter
   Color: Red

2) Sacral Chakra – Represents the ability to be open to new people and experiences Location: Lower abdomen
   Emotional Issues: Concerns related to pleasure, abundance, well-being, and sexuality
   Color: Orange

3) Solar Plexus Chakra – Represents how we feel about ourselves and our abilities to manage our lives
   Location: Upper abdomen
   Emotional Issues: Concerns related to self-worth, self-confidence, and self-esteem
   Color: Yellow

4) Heart Chakra – Represents our ability to give and receive love
   Location: Center of the chest
   Emotional Issues: Concerns related to love, joy, and inner peace
   Color: Green

5) Throat Chakra – Represents our ability to communicate
   Location: Throat
   Emotional Issues: Concerns related to communication, self-expression, and the truth
   Color: Blue

6) Third Eye Chakra (Brow Chakra) – Represents our ability to focus on and see the big picture
   Location: The brow and that part of the forehead that is between the eyes

Emotional Issues: Concerns related to intuition, imagination, wisdom, and decision-making
Color: Indigo

7) Crown Chakra – The highest chakra, the crown chakra represents our ability to be fully connected spiritually
Location: Top of the head
Emotional Issues: Concerns related to beauty and the divine, our connection to spirituality, and bliss
Color: Violet and purple

Seven Chakras research (Internet)

Resources

Healers
Penney Leyshon: www.Penneyleyshon.com
Janice Zwail: www.starluta.com
Abdi Assadi: Abdiassadi.com

Teachers
Shellee Rae (shamanic practitioner): http://www.shel-leerae.com/index.html
Craig Holliday: http://www.craigholliday.com/index.php/about
Jon Bernie: http://www.jonbernie.org/

Films
Wake Up, the Film featuring Jonas Elrod: http://wakeupthefilm.com/

Books
The Evolutionary Energy in Man by Gopi Krishna
A Gift of Healing by Penney LeyShon
The Kundalini Experience by Lee Sannella, Ph.D.
Shadows on the Path by Abdi Assidi
The Tibetan Book of the Dead

Ulster Plantation references – Wikipedia
Cromwell in Ireland references – History Ireland, Globalre-search.org
Peace line wall references – Wikipedia
General Irish history facts – Wikipedia

Kundalini references and various information
Hinduwebsite.com
Adichakti.org

About the Author

The youngest of five children Adrian Clarke was born and raised in West Belfast and grew up amidst violence between the IRA and the British army. As a youth and into his late twenties, Clarke grappled with the demons of alcoholism, PTSD, and depression that lead him to attempted suicide. Through a 12-step recovery process, he found freedom and happiness pursuing a spiritual way of life.

In 2007, an immigrant and former New York ironworker, his spiritual path took an unexpected turn when he experienced a tumultuous spiritual awakening that flooded his being with energy, shaking him to the core. *Living Hell – Living Heaven* chronicles Clarke's struggle to come to terms with the sometimes uncontrollable energy that still courses through him. Today, Clarke is a motivational speaker and gives talks around the U.S. He also specializes in one-on-one counseling for those who are having personal awakenings, particularly traumatic Kundalini, helping them learn about what they are going through.

Facebook = http://www.facebook.com/Adrian.clarke1
Twitter = @ adrianclarke74

41801587R00130

Made in the USA
Middletown, DE
24 March 2017